To Lee Ann ~
  Blessings and best
wishes to a special
woman — I know this
because your father
is so special to me.
      Joan Utda

At the Water's Edge

God's grace in everyday life

Joan Uda

AT THE WATER'S EDGE
GOD'S GRACE IN EVERYDAY LIFE

ISBN 13: 978-0-9798270-0-6
ISBN 10: 0-97987270-0-0
Library of Congress Control Number: 2007937180

Edited by Lowell M. Uda
Designed by Lowell T. Uda
Cover Photo by Warren W. McAllister
Back Cover Photo used courtesy of the Independent Record,

Helena, Montana
Printed in the State of Montana, U.S.A.

RICE
UNIVERSE
PUBLISHING

P.O. Box 1065
East Helena, MT 59635
www.riceuniverse.net

Contents

4

FRUITS OF THE SPIRIT, PAGE 67

5

THE POLITICAL IS SPIRITUAL, PAGE 89

6

TELL ME THE STORIES, PAGE 111

7

COMMUNITY MATTERS, PAGE 131

~Table of Contents~

8

RESTORED TO NEW LIFE, PAGE 151

9

SEASONS OF DISCOVERY, PAGE 171

10

HOLY HAPPINESS, PAGE 195

Preface

The photo on the cover of this book is of me, taken on a California beach by my father. It was in 1943 or 44, during the brief time while he was in training at Camp Hahn in Riverside, an Army installation that in 1976 became the site of the Riverside National Cemetery.

I've always loved this old picture of me. I see it as somehow capturing the person God made me to be. Even at this young age, I often stared far into the distance, wondering. Why were things this way or that? Why did the ocean change colors? I think I nearly drove my mother crazy.

One of my little habits persisted well into grade school. I would hear my mother say a word, something simple like "school" or "boat" or "pole," a word I'd heard and said hundreds, maybe thousands, of times. But one day it would sound unfamiliar to me, as if I'd never heard it before.

"What does 'pole' mean?" I'd ask my mom.

"Pole?" she'd ask, cocking an eye at me.

"Um-hum," I'd say. "Pole."

"Joanie, you know that word," she'd answer.

"No I don't," I'd insist. And I'd ask her to repeat it while I mulled over the sounds and rolled them around in my mouth until I nearly wore them out.

When I was younger, she usually laughed about my word questions. She had a gentle, musical laugh that I loved, and her brown eyes turned even softer and kinder than usual.

When I reached second or third grade, she was tired of my word exercises and would get annoyed. "I've heard you use that word dozens of times," she'd say. "I can't believe you don't know what it means."

It's hard for a child to explain why she doesn't know something her mother thinks she does know or ought to know, especially something basic, something she's clearly known before. I don't know why I'd lose words that way. My best guess is that it happened because of some odd, God-given wiring in my head. Maybe God wanted me to hear things differently and raise questions, and wasn't overly concerned that it might ruffle the adults who loved me.

Or maybe all children are wired this way, and I just had more stamina or stubbornness than some.

When the cover photo was taken, I was at an age when I knew nothing of the furious war raging in Europe, Africa and Asia. It was a war that by some estimates took more than 60 million lives around the world. I only knew that my mom, my daddy and I had recently come to live in a new place, and I loved the beach and the roaring, rippling sea.

As I look at that photo now, I wonder what percentage

of the world's people have led such a privileged life as I. Yes, my daddy went off to war. And after three years he came home alive to Mom and me. During his time overseas, he suffered only minor physical damage to his back. He was riding in the back of a jeep when a steep rut threw him out.

The injuries to his soul went deeper, and finally only left him, I believe, shortly before he died. For as long as I lived at home, if I got up in the middle of the night to visit the bathroom, the moment I opened my bedroom door my dad would charge out of his bedroom in his underwear, eyes glazed with a trancelike expression on his face. Then he'd see me, or maybe recognize me, and his face would relax.

"It's just me, Daddy," I'd say.

"Goodnight," he'd murmur and disappear back into his bedroom.

He slept so lightly, and I knew it came from the many months he spent in foxholes on Okinawa and other Pacific islands.

"They'd come in at night," he told me, "the enemy soldiers. You had to wake up at the slightest sound or there'd be one in the foxhole with you and you'd be bayoneted. They were very quiet."

He slept in the jungle for many years. I finally learned not to get up at night when he was home.

He sustained himself in two ways that I know of. Mom

wrote to him almost every day. He wrote home as often as he could. His letters came with little square holes censored and cut out, anything he said that might aid the enemy.

I don't remember Mom sharing those letters with me, though I'm sure she did. When I was in high school I found them in an old footlocker in our basement. I read them all.

Dad's letters were beautiful, sweeping descriptions and sensitive narratives. He longed for home and wrote love poems to my mother.

I would never have dreamed that my father's soul harbored a poet, and I never saw the poet in him after that. But all his life he bore the injuries to his soul with dignity and fortitude.

The world as I see it now is saturated with war, famine and poverty. I do not write often of these things because my experience of them is indirect, the child who waited in Iowa and cried, "When is Daddy coming home?" My Daddy was my hero.

After the American victory on Okinawa, the war passed elsewhere and my father was ordered to stay behind and care for the war-ravaged Okinawan civilians. In photo after photo, the children look emaciated and numb with fear. "What will happen to us now?" they must have been wondering, as they watched these strange Yankee soldiers building barracks and setting up cots and desks for them.

My wonderful father built not only houses and schools for the children, but he also built playgrounds with swings and slides.

"Children need to play," he explained, "so we did the best we could. We scrounged old tires and everything we could however we could. And then we had to remind them how to play."

I was the well-fed six-year-old who wept over his photos of the starving Okinawan children.

What I write is grounded in my own faith and largely in my own personal history. I tell these little stories because I believe holding my life up to the light of the Bible and the religious experience of others heals my spirit, shows me who God made me to be and helps me to grow.

Writing about these experiences teaches me bit by bit to delve deeper. So much is forgotten, so much hidden. When I was twenty-five I remembered very little about my childhood. Random memories might flash through my mind, but I was never quite able to hold and explore them.

It was, I understand now, a kind of fear-induced amnesia like a heavy, damp curtain that I am slowly pulling back. There is still much that I don't remember or can't write about. But in telling these small stories as truthfully as I can, God gives me the insight and grace to go further. I am working, as Jesus says, to get the log out of my own eye. It seems to be a giant sequoia.

I love that early photo of myself because, as I uncover the truths of my life, I find that I am still that questioning, dreamy child gazing over the wide Pacific.

For many years I couldn't remember her very well, and I could not love her fully. Now those memories are surfacing. And as I gaze at that child, I can almost hear the waves, smell the salty tang of the sea, and feel the sand between my toes.

— *Joan Uda, 2007*

AT
THE
WATER'S
EDGE

FACING WHAT'S HIDDEN

The essays in this book were written during the past two years, starting about nine months after I experienced open-heart surgery for a badly regurgitating aorta.

The surgery changed me. Though I'd always believed that I loved and appreciated life whole-heartedly, I learned during my recuperation that there are vistas of appreciation and love far beyond what I'd known. It also taught me that, however far I may have come, my journey has barely begun.

I'm finding that one of my grandest temptations of spiritual life is to think I'm there. Wherever there is, that's where I am. "I once was lost but now am found."

I sing it with gusto. "Was blind but now I see." Right.

In fact, the layers of spiritual arrogance I've discovered in myself are awesome. Comic at times, but at others they're soul-warping. Spiritual arrogance can masquerade as anything from excessive humility to a delusional God-like knowing of all there is to know.

Feminist theologians have pointed out that excessive humility is more a woman's sin than a man's. It can lead to a victimized posture that is unappealing and can be used for manipulation and control. Been there — not often — but been there.

In women's defense is that I and most older women and many younger were reared to be subservient. "Joanie," I remember my mom's voice, "you're going to have to get over that behavior," which was endless questions and rambunctious antics, "if you're ever going to please a man."

Her voice was soft and a little desperate. It was her job to teach me my place in grownup life. My place in my inevitable future, marriage.

And I was in seventh grade, beginning to rebel at the life I saw unrolling before me. I didn't fully get what she was saying to me, but I did understood that who I was, a child of persistent questioning and an often wild sense of humor, wasn't okay.

These were the days when women went to college to find the right husband and then, if the money was tight, dropped out and got a job to earn her PhT, "putting hubby through." It was okay for my mom to work as a school librarian to make ends meet while my father was overseas. But then, when he came home, she had to quit to become a fulltime wife and mother. "Career" women were déclassé or worse.

Is there any wonder that so many of those attitudes have lingered, in me, in other women and society at large?

Once a woman said to me, in one of the churches I pastored, "Oh, I'm so unworthy. My husband doesn't love me and how can God love me? I know how unlovable I am." Mired in self-blame and self-pity, she couldn't seem to dig her way out of it.

I recognized her feelings. Occasionally even now I feel unloved by God and everybody. It's all too easy to move from there to, "I am unworthy of being loved." In me that is the three-month-old infant in the orphanage who was at last adopted into a loving home but never quite left behind those painful early experiences.

Over many months I reassured this woman, as I reassure myself, that God's love is open, without reservation. I told her that God loves her as a good parent does, exactly as she is. It's complete, all-embracing, a love with no regard whatsoever to any limitations or failings she might have.

I know this love in God toward me, and I've seen it in myself and others toward our children. It is the most real thing in the world if we open ourselves to receive it.

Another form of spiritual arrogance is seeing one's self as spiritually superior. Maybe as closer to God or more like Jesus, or as having discovered all the important questions about the life of faith.

Spiritual superiority has almost endless guises, and I confess that it can pop up any time in me in the most obnoxious ways. This is an even harder spiritual struggle for me than excessive humility. There are so many pieces of it that I am nowhere near to sorting it out. It is the core of my prayer life as I write this, and I am full of hope.

I am blessed by being married to a man who, after forty-four years of marriage, shows not a shred of spiritual arrogance. We're good friends, he and I, and I think I'd see it if it were in him.

I am even more blessed that he is entirely forgiving, and patiently helps me, more by example than anything else, to see these badly broken places in myself that still contain so much pain.

Pain is, I believe, what underlies spiritual arrogance. It's the kind of pain that contorts lives, separates us from our Lord and Savior Jesus Christ by not allowing us to be open to his gentle ministrations. It's the depth of pain that causes us to block the Holy Spirit's efforts to cleanse our souls and draw us closer to the One we worship.

These pages reveal some of this pain, the parts I've been able to face.

There is much, much more. I think if I could be wholly honest, if I told the whole truth as my best self yearns to, the very process would scare me half to death.

It goes back to my beginnings, I the orphanage child

mentioned above, born to an unmarried mother whose name I don't know, adopted at almost three months. And yet I've never been willing to search for this unknown mother. On the surface this unwillingness presents itself as lack of interest.

I wonder if that's because I've always had a "real" mom, my adoptive mother, who supplied me with such abundant love, attention and nurturing. Because of her, and my dad too, I've felt no lack of good parenting nor any need to search.

Yet maybe that's not the whole story. Why would I not want to find this woman whose flesh and blood I am, who carried me under her heart for all those months of gestation? Is it possible that even now I harbor anger at her for deserting me?

Again I discover that there's more. No matter how far I delve, there's always more. Boiling inside me are things I cannot yet mention. I'm afraid of them.

And yet as Jesus says, the truth will out. "For nothing is hidden that will not be disclosed, nor is anything secret that will not become known and come to light." Luke 8:17.

Family therapists and counselors have understood for decades that secrets make us sick. My lifelong friend Carol A. had a dad who was an alcoholic. She spent most of her adult life trying to deal with the effects of his alcoholism on her and the rest of her family.

Jesus wants us to face what is hidden in ourselves. What is hidden in me. I've discovered that doing this work is slow, frightening and piercing.

And then I grow. God reveals new vistas. Where I have come so far is revealed in this book.

So many people have aided me on my journey. First are Warren and Alice McAllister, my parents. Most sustaining and nurturing is my life's best friend, my husband Lowell Masato Uda. My children, Cari French, Michael Uda, Elizabeth Uda and Lowell Takeo Uda educated me about what is important in life almost from the ground up. My children's spouses, Roger French, Cathy Uda and Frank Massman, and our five grandchildren, I am blessed to say, continue this good work.

And then there are those special friends whose grace and goodness taught me so much about love and friendship. Among them are Carol Mitchell, Carol Knight, John and Pat Baker-Batsel, Dave Andersen and Mary Harsh, David and Vickie Orendorff, Delwin Brown, Dana Wilbanks, Bob and Polly Holmes, Rick Newby and Liz Ganz.

My family and friends have patiently read manuscripts, made comments and supported me. To this community of teachers and saints, and others — of whom not one, I suspect, would admit to being a saint — I owe my life and this book.

I owe a special debt to Dave Shors, John Doran and Rich Myers of Helena's Independent Record, where many of these pieces first appeared as a weekly column. I am so grateful.

~At the Water's Edge~

HAND IN HAND

1

Powdered Sugar

owell and I met when we were grad students at the University of Iowa and I was part-time secretary to Paul Engle, founder of the Iowa Writers' Workshop. My life was chaotic. I was a working mother supporting myself and two small children, carrying a full-time student load. I probably wasn't doing a great job at any of it, but we survived.

The office was in an old WWII quonset hut, squeezed beside the Iowa River near the student union. That September a slender, handsome young man from Hawaii came in and asked me to go to the park with him to feed the ducks.

Instead we encountered a gaggle of geese, who were deeply offended when we ran out of bread. That day I learned that geese hiss. They chased us all the way to our car. I've never trusted geese since.

Lowell and I dated a few months and then one bitterly cold day in December he stopped by the office to ask me out for coffee. Enthusiastically I grabbed my coat.

We had coffee and donuts. I chose powdered sugar — I loved the explosive little way powdered sugar melts in my mouth. We talked intently about many things.

Then he looked at me and started laughing.

"What's so funny?" I demanded indignantly. He just kept laughing.

I looked down and saw powdered sugar all over the front of my dark blue wool coat, even down my arms. I didn't want to imagine how my face looked. I was mortified but refused to show it.

"Any woman who enjoys her food so much is the one for me," he said later. He saw how much I loved life. And by then I was enchanted by his kindness, intelligence, and the way he treated my children. One day we were on the footbridge over the river, my son riding on his shoulders, my daughter walking hand in hand between us. A woman came along and said, "You all look so happy."

Now he and I seem like the perfect match. At the time, though, I can't believe Lowell had any idea what he was getting into. Maybe he just loved a challenge. I'd been abused by my ex and was slowly recovering my energy and self-respect. I worked hard and was usually exhausted, feeling that I was holding things together by my fingernails. I remember a night the children spent throwing up. I comforted them through the wee hours, changing and washing sheets. Then my antiquated dryer died. I put the children to bed on towels and blankets, collapsed on my tiny living room floor and sobbed until dawn.

So much seemed against us when we got married. We were broke, heady about our studies, and fairly ignorant about marriage and child-rearing. On our behalf, we tried hard, with lots of love.

I like to believe that God looked at us and thought: these two can make a good life together if they'll grow up and put me at the center of their marriage. And yes, God stayed with us through all those years of struggle, becoming our number one teacher, referee and cheerleader.

Groundhog Day

My husband and I recently celebrated our forty-third wedding anniversary. We married on Groundhog Day, which in my opinion was the perfect day for us. I remember a shy, simply gorgeous young Japanese man, born and brought up in Hawaii, reared Mormon, who kissed me so hard the first time that he bruised my lips. "Ha, not much experience," I recall thinking.

And there I was, a frightened but determined young woman from Iowa, reared Methodist and the divorced mother of two small children. When Lowell called his parents to tell them about me, his father was silent and his mother wept. His mother saw, I believe, that life for us wouldn't be easy. I wasn't Japanese or Mormon, I'd flunked Marriage One and had two little children. Poor, shocked Mom. Poor us.

When Lowell and I went to meet my parents, I remember my mother mostly trying to calm my dad. Dad was a WWII veteran of the Pacific campaign. He hauled out the authentic Japanese sword that he'd taken from a captured Japanese officer on Okinawa, and waved it around, filling the room with "you people" this and "J#@" that. My dad was a very loving man, but this match, right then, was too much for him. Both he and Mom came to love my husband dearly, but not that night when Dad was so upset and all I wanted was to flee.

Our parents had reason to be concerned. I saw Lowell as nearly perfect and he handled our parents well, but I recall myself as insecure, inexperienced and self-centered.

Enter Groundhog Day, the movie. Bill Murray plays an obnoxious weatherman visiting Punxsutawney, Pa., to find out if groundhog Punxsutawney Phil will see his shadow. Murray and Andie McDowell get snowed in and have to spend the night. Murray wakes up in the morning to discover that the very same day has recurred. Over and over. After his initial horror and dismay wear off, he finds that he can learn new things, and in the process he changes himself. He turns from an egocentric blowhard into the warm, gifted human being who all along was hidden inside the obnoxious façade.

Lowell and I never actually had to repeat the same day again and again, but we surely had plenty of ups and downs to learn from. We had close calls with separation, but we persevered.

Our love now reminds me of that finely forged Japanese sword where the steel is thrust into the fire and beaten over and over again. It is finely honed and tempered, unbreakable, not even, I believe, by death.

A friend recently said in a sermon: "Common wisdom advises that if you want to do something great, start with greatness, or, said inversely, 'Garbage in, garbage out.'" His point was that common wisdom isn't God's wisdom. God doesn't start with greatness. God creates it from the commonplace. God created humankind from dirt: Adam, the earth-man. God took two confused, immature young people, and between them forged a great love that is forever. I call that a miracle.

Just a Closer Walk

A reservoir near our house is one of my favorite places. I recall a July evening some years ago when my husband and I were preparing to move to Denver so that he could enter seminary. We took our young black cockapoo Ipolani to the reservoir.

We parked on the south side, the side furthest from the highway, and we rode our new bikes, made like the old-fashioned kind with fat tires and upright handlebars. We headed toward the far end where we assumed the trail continued around the reservoir. And, because nobody else was there, we let Ipo run loose.

It was already dusk when we arrived, but that didn't bother us. We thought we knew where we were going. Very rapidly dusk turned to inky darkness, no lights anywhere, and there we were, unable to see, no flashlight, no leash for Ipo, scrambling through underbrush, hoping not to fall into the water, working our way around the end of the reservoir to the highway.

By the time we reached the road, I was cold, worn out and half angry. I recall that stretch of highway as being very narrow then, barely two lanes, with steep rock on one side and almost no shoulder on the other. It was frighteningly dark. Lowell rode his bike, carrying squirmy Ipo under his arm, and I followed, muttering how I hoped no vehicle would rush up behind and splatter us.

Finally we reached the main entrance and hurried across the causeway to our car, our adventure over.

A few afternoons ago Lowell and I took a half-hour walk at the reservoir. The temperature was about forty degrees and the sky was bright blue, rimmed with low-lying cumulus clouds. The ice on the reservoir had thinned and there was much open water, though most of the shoreline was snowpack.

The day was brisk, billowy and quiet, with few people. The wind was at our backs as we left our car, and in spite of the cold I tasted a tang of spring in the air.

This time God seemed very near to me as we walked. Lowell and I didn't talk much, and I enjoyed a kind of companionable solitude with him, my spirit feeling alone and at rest though my body was moving. At the same time I had, very silently, a remarkable experience.

Something about the place, I don't know what, sent a kind of rejoicing into my blood, as if the God-in-everything that the Apostle Paul speaks of in Acts 17:28, the God in whom we live and move and have our being, was flowing into me from the sky, water, trees, earth, meeting as kindred the God-in-everything that lives in me. I felt so connected to God and to the place that even the cold wind was more pleasant than not. I wanted to keep walking and walking until either my excitement quieted or I was too tired to move.

Finally we turned back. As we climbed into the car and left, I felt physically and spiritually refreshed. I'd been under the weather for a few days, and our walk had made those feelings vanish. It was, I'm convinced, just because of a few minutes that felt like intimacy with God.

Though I didn't recognize it at the time, that same God accompanied us during our earlier adventure. But since then I've opened my life to God and God has lifted my eyes to new life. I've beheld the wonder of a God who walks with us, holds us close, and shows us the blessings of a blustery late winter day.

Keeping What Matters

I didn't grow up in the Great Depression of the 1930s, but my parents did. I was taught that you made do, used things up, gave away what was still useful, or did without. No wonder I cling to so many things.

My closets and drawers are brimming. In my closet are storage boxes heaped with inspirational books once belonging to my mom and grandmother. From "A Heap o' Living" by Edgar A. Guest, dated 1916:

~Hand in Hand~

'Tis better to have tried in vain,
Sincerely striving for a goal,
Than to have lived upon the plain
An idle and timid soul.

Edgar Guest is mostly forgotten, but this was one of my Grandma Carlton's favorite books. How can I part with it? Every so often I pull the boxes down and read a few pages. These books are still "improving," if I have the patience for them. Will any of my children want them? Grandchildren? I can't consign them to a landfill.

I have a box of my dad's tie clasps and cuff links, all rusty now, and a desk plaque carved in the shape of his name. I have his high school diploma, his navy blue beret that he bought on a trip to France with Mother while I was in high school, and his Kiwanis "Man of the Year" award. These things aren't going to the landfill any time soon, either.

So I walk around the house and grumble about clutter, shredding old tax returns and new credit card offers, muttering about junk mail and feeling overwhelmed with the need to deal with so much stuff.

We've taken truckloads of recyclables to our favorite charity, and bags and bales of rubbish to the dump. We've given things to our kids. At last the house feels more peaceful, less cluttered — not quite there yet but closer. The remnants continue migrating toward the garage, where they wait until we move them out.

So do I send the kids' old report cards to live with them — to clutter up their houses? Will they think I don't love them if their grade reports from the seventies arrive on their doorsteps? After all, I'm keeping their childhood ceramics, my favorite triceratops with broken horns and the red-and-gray striped whatsis that I never did figure out.

It's easy to get rid of pure junk. But these special things radiate love to me. When I look at them, they bring back departed elders and tiny children who are now thriving adults with lives and children of their own.

My task is to sort what matters from what doesn't, to mercilessly get rid of what doesn't and to preserve what's good and meaningful.

In a way, this is like my spiritual journey. Rediscover and claim what's good and meaningful, and give up what isn't. It reminds me of returning to the church after I'd been gone for many years. When I let go my pride, phony self-sufficiency and other spiritual clutter, I found God.

I have to admit, it's a worthy exchange.

Yellowstone in Winter

Recently Lowell and I went snowmobiling in Yellowstone Park. We never did that before, and I've always had more negative than positive associations with snowmobiles. Aren't they loud, polluting and dangerous?

I formed those associations decades ago, when we lived in Missoula and took visiting friends up to Lolo Pass. While we were chasing our other children, our friends put our ten-year-old son on a snowmobile. The first we knew of it was when we saw our boy driving a snowmobile across a huge open field. As we ran toward him, the snowmobile overturned.

There was our son lying in the snow, unmoving. The ambulance ride back to Missoula was one of the most harrowing moments of my life, especially when the driver turned on the siren.

After head-to-toe X rays, our son turned out to be fine, only a few little bumps. We thought maybe he was paralyzed with fear, probably over what we'd say about him getting on that snowmobile. It never occurred to us he'd do that.

So you could have knocked me over with a snowflake several weeks ago when we saw a brochure offering snowmobile packages in Yellowstone. We looked at each other saying, "Yes, why not?"

Amazed at ourselves yet never wavering in our resolve, we signed up. We were so excited. All went well until the morning of the ride when we had to walk two blocks from our hotel to the snowmobile departure point. The snowmobile suits that we rented weighed at least a ton, and there was snow on the streets that we had to wade through. If I say I was scared I'd be lying. It was more like terror.

I stumbled along with tears in my eyes, wanting to turn back. Lowell laughed and said I looked like a two-year-old bundled up in her first snowsuit who falls down and just lies there bawling, unable to move. My determination kicked in and we made it to the departure point with time to spare.

Yellowstone in winter is breathtakingly lovely. I rode behind my sweetheart for sixty-five miles to and from Old Faithful, a regular bobble-headed doll, icy cold and utterly exhilarated. Seeing the park this way inspires prayers of gratitude. We stopped often, usually for animals either on or near the road, mainly bison, elk, coyotes and trumpeter swans.

During our two-hour lunch break at Old Faithful, I napped in front of a roaring fire for an hour. Nine and a half weeks after hip surgery, I had ignored my fears and accepted the challenge.

The next day we took a snow coach to the Grand

Canyon of the Yellowstone, a longer and warmer trip. On balance I prefer the snow coach, but I wouldn't have missed my snowmobile day for anything.

It's as if God gave me back my zest in life. Seeing Yellowstone that way was something I never thought I could do, and I did it. I believe God smiles to see us having so much fun.

Don't Lose Touch

I went to Virginia to see Dave, our eldest grandson. He's seventeen, a high school senior, getting ready to plunge into young adult life on his own. His mother, our daughter, works hard to help him acquire the skills he'll need.

One day he said, "Mom, why do you want me to go away to college? Don't you want me here?"

She said, "I want you here very much. It's for your own good because you need to do certain things in order to grow up." She is very smart.

Three summers ago Dave hung out in the woods a lot making things go boom. So his mom got him involved in NOLS, the National Outdoor Leadership School. He has since taken two month-long NOLS hiking trips with kids his own age into remote wilderness areas, first in Wyoming and then in Alaska. His developing leadership skills show in most things he does.

He got a job bussing tables at a white-tablecloth fish restaurant. After his Alaska trip, Dave's employer took him back. "I held his job," the boss said to my daughter. "He sees things that need to be done and does them without being asked. Even when a customer pukes, Dave cheerfully cleans it up while the others gag."

This is the boy who injures himself and watches the doctor put stitches in his arm. The doctor whispered to my daughter, "Nobody ever watched me sew them up before."

My first day in Virginia Dave came home early from school with noro-virus, a nasty flu-like bug. He slept a while and came downstairs hungry.

"Try a few sips of water," his mom said. "If you keep that down, have some broth." Instead he peeled a grapefruit, stuffed it in his mouth and soon ran for the bathroom. Then he stretched out his six-foot-three, string-bean frame on the couch with his head in his mom's lap to have her rub his head.

Later his mom said, "Do you remember that your grandpa Lowell taught you to love grapefruit when you were tiny?"

"Yup," he said. "He taught me to gut fish, too. On my NOLS trips I was the only kid who knew how."

One night while I was there, Dave invited his younger

brother Ben and me to dinner where he works. He insisted on paying though I offered. "Grandma," he said proudly, "I have a discount." What a great evening.

He's a remarkable boy, loving, bright, energetic and sweet. I can't bear to let him drift out of my life, so I went to Virginia to renew our bond. Watching him, who he is and is becoming, and the quality of parenting he and his brother receive from both parents, I am thrilled.

To say I'm proud of him is an understatement. I'm so happy at all signs of a real relationship between him and his Grandpa Lowell and me.

Don't lose touch. Our children and grandchildren are our profoundest legacy, our greatest response to God's promises.

Flowers for Leila

Years ago a dear friend asked me to visit her. She lived in another town and she insisted that I come to see her. She had something she needed to do and she wanted me with her.

She wouldn't tell me what it was but she piqued my curiosity, so I went.

I pulled into her driveway at four o'clock on a beautiful spring afternoon. She suggested that we get into her car.

"This last weekend," she said, "I learned from my nana about an aunt I never knew I had. I never even heard her name before."

My friend's grandmother was very elderly by then. She lived in the city where my friend grew up. I'd met her a couple of times when my friend took me to her house.

We drove to the city's oldest cemetery, a place of winding roads, arching elms and huge evergreens.

"You already know," my friend said, "that Nana isn't very well. She thinks she won't live much longer. She told me about her daughter Leila, my aunt, who got pregnant when she was nineteen. That was in 1934, and it was a terrible thing."

It was a familiar story. Unmarried girls who got pregnant in those days were viewed as fallen women, sinful, maybe even unredeemable. Most of them never told their stories, but those who did spoke of humiliation, emotional and sometimes physical abuse.

The story was dear to my own heart because, from what little I know of her, one of those women was my biological mother. I was born in 1939 to a young woman who, according to my adoptive father, was a "chorus girl."

My friend said, "My grandfather threw Leila out of the house and told her never to come back. No one was ever allowed to mention her again. She didn't exist. I called my mother about this, but she was little then and doesn't even remember Leila's name."

"Nana learned later," my friend continued, "that Leila moved to this town, got a job in a grocery store and died a few months later in childbirth. Nana never could learn anything about Leila's child or what happened to it."

We searched for an hour before we found what we thought might be Leila's grave. It was tucked away in a weedy, unkempt area near the machinery shed. There was no marker. It was as if she'd been rejected as much in death as in life.

"I'm going to put up a headstone for her," my friend said. "It doesn't matter that we can't be sure this is Leila's grave."

And it didn't. We knew she was buried somewhere nearby, and I couldn't help thinking of the woman who gave birth to me. I hoped she had gone on to make a good life, as good as the one my adoptive parents gave me.

My friend and I were both crying by then. "Do you suppose things are any better now?" my friend asked.

"I hope so," I said.

And we went to buy a bouquet for Leila's grave.

Angelica's Illness

I wouldn't call Angelica a health nut — but she's close.

She exercises vigorously many times a week and gets her family exercising too. She prepares food that is nutritionally excellent. She measures portions, uses only heart-healthy oils and concocts delicious desserts from egg whites.

At fifty, Angelica is a size eight, the same size she was at twenty. The few pounds she put on with her three children she took right off.

Angelica's husband still has a youthful figure too. He's a banker, and as the years go by he watches his associates crumble with heart disease, diabetes and cancer.

He grumped for years about Angelica's family health program, but now, says Angelica, "He gets it."

Of course there are days when he and their teenage son just have to break ranks and hit a fast food place. Their boy comes home saying, "That food rocks!" Privately, though, he'll tell you his mom's a great cook.

But Angelica says her husband always looks slightly queasy after the burger and fries. "I think I wrecked it for him," she laughs.

Then Angelica got breast cancer. It wasn't in her health program. Her initial feelings of devastation and anger soon turned to depression.

I thought she was grieving for her lost understanding of things. I wondered if, in her pursuit of healthful living, she'd forgotten that no matter how well we take care of ourselves, we don't have ultimate control. So many things can go wrong with the human body.

Two years later Angelica's doing well, I'm happy to say. She had excellent medical care and now tests cancer free. She's back to her health program, as vigorous as ever.

But some days I hear a certain sadness in her voice. She's not particularly religious, and I think her cancer caught her in her all-too-human self-sufficiency.

"By my own self," I hear my grandchildren say, as I once said, and so did our own children.

Part of our national understanding of ourselves is that we are ruggedly independent, individualistic, a pull-yourself-up-by-your-own-bootstraps kind of people. My parents, especially my dad, taught me to be self-sufficient and independent. All the time, that was, except when I was taking orders from him.

But I wasn't well-trained in interdependence, the kind of give-and-take that makes good partnerships, good marriages and great communities.

It took me many years to lay down my independence and self-sufficiency before God and cry, "Oh Lord, I need you. Every day I need you. In my getting up, all day long and when I lie down at night. Oh Lord, I need you."

I tried to talk to Angelica about this, and she suddenly had to get off the phone.

Yes, I've been in that place too, unwilling to accept help from God or anybody.

When she's ready, God will be there waiting and loving her, ready to lift her burden, support her and give her inner peace, just as God did for me.

In God's time, and in Angelica's time.

Be Mine, Valentine

My sweetheart and I have celebrated more than four decades of marriage. This year we stretched our anniversary out for a week. On the actual day, we had a special dinner, just the two of us, and a week later we went dancing with friends.

Before we were married, the minister sat us down and said, "Marriage is like two stones grinding together until there's a perfect fit." The image I had was of two big stones whacking chunks off each other. Not too romantic, I thought.

My intended saved the moment by saying, "Oh, no, marriage is like a dance." Yes, people learning to glide and sway, twirling responsively together, much more how we both wanted to think of marriage.

Like most people in long-term relationships, we've seen a lot together. Life-threatening illnesses and personal catastrophes, job and career changes, disappointments that seemed big at the time and faded with the years. And of course the overwhelming number of incredible moments: our children's births and so many things in their lives, our own learning how to love each other, and our ordinations and ministries.

Life with my husband is so rich that I cannot imagine more happiness than to be with him. Which is strange because I notice that even when we're both home, we're rarely in the same room unless it's mealtime. Usually we're doing separate things, and yet we're wonderfully, marvelously aware of each other. It's remarkable.

He is my valentine for all eternity.

Which brings me to the inevitable: one day we will part. No one can know which of us will go first. Sometimes we almost argue about it. "Me first." "No, me first." Nobody wants to be left.

Now we are discussing what to do with our bodily remains when that time comes. Burial? Cremation? Both of us lean toward the latter. It's more environmentally friend-ly, we think, but then comes the question of whether we park our cremains somewhere that our children can go, if they wish, and think, "Well, what's left of their earthly beings is here." Or do we get scattered in some fine spot? My preference is Grinnell Lake in Glacier Park with the grizzlies and fierce, wild winters.

What all long-time married people know is that this earthly life together doesn't last forever. The blessing is the sure and certain knowledge in Christ that this life is not all there is.

As the Apostle Paul so beautifully puts it, "For I am convinced that neither death, nor life, nor angels, nor rulers, nor things present, nor things to come, nor powers, nor height, nor depth, nor anything else in all creation, will be able to separate us from the love of God in Christ Jesus our Lord." Romans 4:38-39.

For us believers, says Paul, "We will not all die, but we will all be changed." 1 Corinthians 15:51.

I hope and believe that my valentine and I will share eternity together, in whatever way God pleases. I am certain that love never dies. It dances forever in God's heart.

IN THE GARDEN

2

Red String Beans

Gardening is a theme that runs through my life like a recurring melody. In my childhood the gardens belonged to my grandmothers, my aunts and my parents. My family on my father's side were mostly farmers, and I remember, at age ten, picking string beans with my aunt Carmen in her garden.

In those days all string beans were green.

"I think the beans ought to be red," I said. "Then you could see them under the leaves."

My aunt laughed. Then she told my parents, who laughed too. I couldn't see what was funny.

I've gardened quite a few years now, and my learning curve in the garden is still very high. Should potatoes really be planted on Good Friday? Why? Should peas and beans always be planted in rows running north and south, or is that merely an old wives' tale?

My garden has taught me quite a lot of patience as I've crawled around on my knees pulling weeds or bent over, seemingly for hours, planting tiny seeds. And I've barely begun to learn. In the beginning I had a hard time remembering to put my garden tools away, let alone to clean them. I was always rushing off to the next projects, going three or four directions at once and not getting much done.

Learning patience has helped to slow me down and taught me to pay a different kind of attention. I keep notes of what worked and what didn't, when I planted certain things and how. My notes are sketchy yet helpful. And now I mostly put my tools away, and sometimes even clean them. I like to see them all lined up shiny and waiting for me.

As I slowed down in the garden and learned to focus, an amazing thing happened. I discovered that God is always very near when I'm down on my knees with my hands in the dirt. I simply feel embraced. That is why, I suspect, that it's so hard for me to brush the dirt off, return the tools to their places and go inside. God is in there too, of course, but it isn't quite the same.

The most difficult thing about the garden for me is keeping my energy level up even close to what the garden requires. In every season, the work is always ahead of me, more ground to till, veggies and flowers to plant, weeds to pull, flowers to deadhead, produce to process and store.

It's a wonderful challenge. I love how the garden sets the melody and the rhythm of my spring, summer and fall.

Sun-Kissed

After my parents bought their first house, a tiny two-bedroom bungalow, they always found a spot for a garden. That made sense to me because my father was reared on an Iowa farm, the eldest of eight, and the urge to grow things seemed like second nature to him. His mother tended a huge garden as long as she lived on the farm, and my mother's mother kept a garden that was almost an acre. In those days we often ate ripe, fresh food from the garden, picked only hours before dinner. At the time I didn't appreciate how delicious it was, though now the memories make my mouth water.

My father had quite the green thumb and his garden was always beautiful. My mother's job was more to pick what we ate, clean it and bring it to the table. I remember being impatient as I watched my parents work in their garden. I couldn't understand what they saw in getting their hands all dirty, bending over for what seemed like hours to me or kneeling among the rows of lettuce or tomatoes.

I understand now that my dad's garden was a cherished retreat from his long days as a retail store manager, where every night he'd take the tapes from each cash register and meticulously record the day's sales so he could compare totals with yesterday's, last month's and last year's. These days this is probably done entirely with computers. Then it was painstakingly hand-written in tiny ledger columns.

After all his closing chores were done at the store, Dad would hurry home and disappear into his bedroom. There he'd shed his silky business suit, his conservative tie and white shirt, and soon emerge in his old Army fatigues. In those days he worked very long hours six days a week. In the garden on his knees he looked happier than at almost any other time I saw him.

My current four-by-eight foot raised beds seem puny in comparison to the gardens of my childhood, yet I'm astonished each year how my little raised plots produce so much to eat with relatively minimal effort on my part. In April we still eat frozen veggies that I put up in the fall. It's a garden miracle.

My dear Aunty-Mom Helen, my mother's sister and my dad's second wife after Mom died, once gave me a garden plaque called "The Kiss of the Sun":

The kiss of the sun for pardon,
The song of the birds for mirth,

One is nearer God's heart in a garden
Than anywhere else on earth.

I am blessed and frequently sun-kissed in my garden.

My Greenhouse Effect

In spring there's always plenty to do in my greenhouse. I don't mind because I love it there. The greenhouse is small, but it's plenty big enough for me. More would be too much. I've planted six flats, everything from purple basil to red-hot Mexican sunflowers. My cucumbers and morning glories are tall enough that I've transplanted some of them into individual pots.

The greenhouse is a beauty. One side has a work bench and storage, and the other is sloped, with real greenhouse polycarbonate for glass, and a wide, low bench for the plants. It sits right beside our veggie garden.

Lowell built the greenhouse two summers ago. I didn't get to do a fall planting that year, because we took a long trip to see our east coast daughter and her family.

Within a month after we returned, I learned about my heart condition and surgery followed a few weeks later. All last year my lovely greenhouse sat idle.

No enclosed space around here sits empty for long,

though, and soon the greenhouse was crammed to the rafters with tools, garden and lawn gear, buckets of bird seed and just plain junk. We stuffed in everything that didn't fit elsewhere.

When I got back on my feet I'd stare at that greenhouse, feeling guilty. Lowell built it so beautifully, and here I was, making absolutely no use of it. I'd wanted it so much, and now it seemed like the grown-up equivalent of the Atari that, many Christmases ago, our ten-year-old son just had to have. Within a month he'd swapped it with a friend for something else. Was my greenhouse going a similar way, turning into a costly, labor-intensive hunk of junk in the yard?

About a month ago I fired myself up and tackled the mess. Lowell came out too, and we sorted, stored and disposed of. We even found a couple of dead mice and went tippy-toeing around for days with our surgical masks and spray bottles of bleach. But now, I'm happy to say, I have a lovely place. As someone once quipped, sometimes I sit there and work, and sometimes I just sit.

The greenhouse offers a great learning process. After drowning some seeds and frying some baby plants, I'm discovering how to monitor sun and shade, temperature, seed depth, and moisture.

At the same time I found myself thinking recently that

I haven't been monitoring my own spiritual health and growth nearly as well. Sometimes I reach a point when my prayers turn perfunctory, and I behave as if I'm too busy for God.

Yet I know only too well that if I become distracted and impatient, my relationship with God grows as thin and feeble as a plant that receives too little sun.

The truth is, a spiritual life requires daily tending and monitoring, just like my plants. God tends me when I pay attention to God. Thank you, greenhouse, for reminding me of this. Now more is growing in there than just my plants. What a wonderful place.

Ah, Spring, Ah, Life

Recently I've been spending time in the garden, in the sunshine with the smells of spring all around me. I cleared winter debris from veggie beds and tumbleweeds from the fences.

Late last fall Lowell planted mesclun and spinach, and the mesclun was only brown, desiccated leaves. But as I lifted the dead spinach leaves, I found new growth. I'm thinking early spinach this year.

We left some green onions in the ground last fall, and they lived but got soft, and they sent out these huge, ferocious root systems that make the soil difficult to break up. I spent hours on that one bed.

The wonderful thing about that bed, other than the fine exercise my arms received from tilling it, was the delicate and definite aroma of onions those roots emitted. My mouth started watering before I recognized why, and I sat for a moment just breathing in their oniony bouquet.

Then I moved to the herb bed. The oregano and thyme smelled delicious as I cut them back, and I received enticing whiffs of basil as I pulled out last year's remnants.

I'm coming to believe that the springtime scents while clearing the beds are reason enough to grow these plants, tantalizing fragrances that awaken all my senses to the wonder of God. I love the touch, smells, taste, sound and beauty of the garden as the young plants spring forth and mature.

Each morning now I wake up wondering if I'll have time to garden today. The work feels effortless to me, because the garden fills me with such deep peace that I enter a kind of timelessness where things move in their own quiet rhythms. I have little control there and I know and like that: the labor is mine, but the place and the results belong to God.

Every year my sense of peace in the garden feels greater. Maybe peace is its best crop. The hours fly when I have my fingers in the dirt, and I'm utterly at ease. I just "am," simple, uncomplicated, with God at my shoulder. I feel in tune with the universe.

God and I talk. In the wind and the sunshine, the smells of freshly-turned earth and last year's herbs, we have deep, mostly silent communications. This is not a time when I do much petitionary prayer, unless someone I know is in great need.

My garden prayers are mostly celebrations. Thank you, God, for this great Earth of ours. Help us to use it wisely and not abuse it. Thank you, God, for growing the life-sustaining plants from the tiny seeds I'll soon put in the ground, and for my faith which springs anew like the mighty mustard tree of the parables.

And thank you most of all, Lord, for your Son Jesus Christ, who loved us so much that he was willing to suffer and die that we might understand who he is and learn to follow him. Thank you, God, thank you for new life.

My Master Gardener

What is there about gardening? I get so excited when my seeds germinate that you'd think I'd done it myself. I drag my husband to where the tiny seedlings poke up, saying, "See, see," like a little kid.

Maybe I love gardening so much because when I'm out there, hands and clothes covered with dirt and mud, I become a child again. I open so wide to the great and small glories of nature that it's common for me to get tears in my eyes at the beauty of a bean or squash plant, the perfection of the bees who come to feast on our garden, or the sheer grandeur of our Montana Big Sky.

I am perfectly at home in my garden, relaxed and untroubled. I rarely worry about anything. When I start worrying, I know it's time to go inside. For me the garden is peace, the kind of perfect peace that all of us need in our lives, that de-stresses and puts us in touch with things that really matter.

In fact, gardening is my favorite form of prayer. God is in my garden, the Master Gardener. I am privileged there to walk and talk with God most openly. In the cold months I miss gardening terribly.

So, since the garden catalogs started arriving before Christmas, I've been having an awful time restraining myself. I know it's too soon. Winter has barely settled in.

But sometimes I open the catalogs. I'm so taken with the Red Lightning Hybrid tomato, a brilliant red with yellow stripes. "Sweet, tangy and with a rich aroma," says the page. But the small print tells me they take 82 days to ripen, longer than I like given our short growing season.

Then there's the Monarda called Violet Queen. The flower has many-petaled blossoms of bright fuchsia, and foliage that looks blue-green in the catalog. Will it thrive here? Our perennial gardens are so full that I have to be selective about adding new plants, and of course I leave space for colorful annuals.

I am so ready to get into the garden. The garden catalogs begin preparing my heart, which sometimes seems as frozen as the soil of my garden.

But it's a couple of months even to plant peas, which do best in cold weather. The seed packets say, "Plant as soon as the soil can be worked." I've always been overly cautious about peas, planting in mid-May. But warmth makes them wilt and stop bearing. This year my peas are going in the ground the moment I can till it.

Patience, I counsel myself. God is out there — and in here, too. But my Master Gardener's presence seems so vital, almost palpable in the garden.

It's no wonder these catalogues speak to me. Come look, they say, just check us out. And oh, it's hard to wait.

The Joy of Staying Put

My husband Lowell says, "You know what we have here? We have a small farm."

I have to agree with him even though our veggie garden isn't that big and our fruit trees and bushes are just starting to bear.

Even so, I'm kind of overwhelmed with our produce. This is our apple tree's first year, and we have hundreds of apples. It's a mountain to be washed, peeled, sliced and frozen.

When Lowell was in seminary we lived for ten months in a small townhouse near Denver. We had a twelve-by-twelve concrete patio surrounded by a six-foot fence.

I planted tomatoes in pots. By July my tomato plants were growing over the fence into the neighbor's patio. The manager said to Lowell, "Your wife needs a garden." I'm sure he meant a garden like the one we have today.

This gardening thing has sneaked into my soul. Now, finally retired and no longer an itinerant, I get to see my fruit trees bear fruit and my perennials grow large and luscious.

There's nothing wrong with planting and moving on. That's what Johnny Appleseed did. It brings life and beauty, not to mention apples, to places that didn't have them before.

Maybe that's why one of my favorite hymns is "Harvest Time":

~In the Garden~

The seeds I have scattered in springtime with weeping,
And watered with tears and with dew from on high;
Another may shout when the harvesters reaping
Shall gather my grain in the sweet by and by.

As people of faith, I believe God asks us to scatter seeds without worrying about who will enjoy the harvest. I think that's part of what Jesus means when he tells us not to worry about what we are to wear, eat or drink.

"Consider the lilies," he says, "how they grow: they neither toil nor spin; yet I tell you, even Solomon in all his glory was not clothed like one of these." Luke 12:27-28.

And yet some part of me has always wanted to come to rest and harvest the apples of the trees we planted and eat the strawberries and raspberries from our own patches. I've ached to see the peonies we put in the ground grow round and full like the perfect harbingers of summer that they are.

So this year I've lost track of how many pints of tomatoes and green beans I've frozen. The delicious homemade grape juice is frozen too and I just might try my hand at jelly. The garden is still jammed with carrots, Swiss chard, beets, potatoes and white radishes, some of them a foot long.

But what if God calls again. "Joan, go and do. . . ."

Do I love my garden more than God? Or will I say,

"Here I am, Lord. Send me."

These days I finally have time to sit quietly and contemplate my many blessings. They are, like our produce, nearly overwhelming. If God gives me a new call, that is good. In the meantime, I'm reveling right here in my garden.

Garden Music

You can see how happy my garden is this year by the way the tomato plants are over four feet tall, a thick jungle of arching leaves and baby tomatoes. This morning I spent an hour trimming non-bearing stems to let in more light and air, and give the fruit more energy. While I worked, I heard the tomato plants singing to me. I felt utterly at peace.

Then I moved on to the raspberries. This year they're bearing, and I went from plant to plant popping berries in my mouth. When I reached the house I had only one berry left. Raspberries always seem to me most delicious straight off the bush.

I filled a basin of snow peas, pulled Chinese cabbage that bolted last week, and picked lettuce for lunch. This year we grew mesclun, a mix of many lettuce varieties. We love a big bowl of it for lunch with our homemade balsamic vinaigrette.

A pair of robins nested in our yard this year, and now

baby is out of the nest. Mom and dad are watching hard for the neighborhood cats, who love to creep amidst the plants. Meadowlarks sing in our garden, and several pairs of bluebirds visit every day and feast on our many insects.

My garden sings to me all the time. When I'm in it, its music fills me with pleasure and tranquility. It's all I can do to drag myself into the house. My study window overlooks a front garden with deep purple sage, white daisies, old-fashioned orange daylilies, yellow California poppies — it sings a siren song. I almost have to tie myself to my chair to keep at work.

One of the things I love most about gardening is the way it makes a place for me and shows me how I fit into God's created world. In the garden I feel very open to God and to the nature around me. Everything, including me, is in its proper order.

I am God's creature too, my garden teaches me. I feel related to all of it, the plants, the birds, the earthworms we so carefully cultivated, the mosquitoes we haven't quite eliminated, the occasional grasshopper, not to mention the deer who haven't found us yet. Gardening teaches me that I neither can nor want to be in charge, and thinking about getting My Way in the garden isn't even a very good joke. The garden has its own rhythms and necessities and I must work cooperatively and lovingly with those. In the garden I become more the person God made me to be.

Garden — hmmm. I seem to recall something about a Garden before Adam and Eve got themselves chased out. Maybe that's why my garden seems like such a holy place to me. God makes it, I don't. I am merely God's servant there, planting, fertilizing, weeding and harvesting.

Life isn't about me, my garden teaches. It's about us. And, thanks to our loving God, it is very, very good.

Late Summer Garden

Russian sage, red and yellow sunflowers, rudbeckia daisies, California poppies, hydrangeas, echinacea, sweet peas and coreopsis are blooming in my garden.

The mums are blazing away, but the asters are barely starting. They'll be glorious a month from now, barring a hard early frost. I'm always amazed by how late they are.

The marigolds, I've noticed, are now pushing out that fabulous swell of color that always presages the end of their season. They glow as if their light comes from inside. It's lovely yet sad because it means that summer is waning.

Our golden beets are sweet and mellow, our tomatoes vine-ripened and juicy, the onions as big as baseballs. The carrots need pulling, and the peas seem almost done, though my husband insists, "No, see. They're putting up new shoots." "Tiny," I grumble. "They won't do anything."

I've been reading recently about contemporary notions of death and how we deal with it. So many people now see death as grotesque and even a bit "unnatural." To them it looks like utter annihilation of the human person.

I don't agree.

The cycle of things is totally natural. To me as a Christian it is part of God's created world — and it is good.

In my garden most things either die back, go underground or lose their leaves and wait. Then spring cycles through again with all its tender green wonder.

I've reached the time in my life when I know there are a finite number of beautiful summer days left to me. That's part of why I have moments of late-summer melancholy. The other part is that all this garden loveliness will soon wither and turn brown.

I learned first as a pastor and then even more profoundly through my open heart surgery — my own brush with dying — to be mostly comfortable with the idea of my own death.

When I go — a long time from now, I hope — I'll leave the people I love, family and friends, including some I've never met. In this life I'll become one of those pale ghosts in old photographs, but by God's grace my descendents will thrive.

And my faith tells me there's more even for me. It isn't about harps and haloes. That's popular culture. I flat don't know what the other side looks like.

But I believe that when we die, we are born anew into God's boundless, eternal love. I believe that no real love ever ends, that God transitions us in the most gentle and grace-filled way we will allow, and that "over there" we are embraced by everyone who has gone before.

Some days this summer I've almost lived outside, and now I can't get enough of these late summer days when the sky is that bona fide Big Sky blue and the air is warm with a chilly zing in it. I love the coat-at-dawn, sleeveless-by-mid-afternoon routine.

There's joy in every season, delight even in melancholy. God made it so, and it is very good.

IN GOD'S IMAGE

3

In the Faces
of Those We Meet

Some years ago Lowell and I were living in Hawaii, surrounded by the ethnic richness of the Islands and our own family. One day I saw an elderly Asian woman walking along the sidewalk toward me and I thought I recognized her. As she drew closer and passed, I was startled by a strong resemblance between her and my maternal grandmother, Edna Mae (Baker) Carlton, who was not Asian and had never been to Hawaii. Grandma lived her life in the American Midwest, with occasional visits to the family who lived in California.

I couldn't keep myself from staring at this woman as long as I could. The resemblance between her and Grandma lay in her thin, kindly facial features that seemed barely wrinkled in spite of her age. It was also in the shape of her head and the way she wore her hair wound up in small braids, and even in her compact body that seemed to radiate energy.

It was like meeting my grandmother in a foreign land. I gazed after the woman for several moments. My head was flooded with images of Grandma, who'd died of uremic poisoning almost ten years earlier. I saw the old wash dresses Grandma wore even while working in the garden. I saw the two of us picking strawberries, tomatoes and peas, and flagging the old jitney down for a ride from her place in Coralville into Iowa City. I even saw my very young self standing beside her on an upturned bucket as she taught me how to make her special chicken and noodles, a dinner I loved.

I was surprised and then thrilled, powerful emotions that imprinted this incident on my memory. I really knew nothing about the Asian woman, but it was the first time, outside our family members, that I had been able to look past our culturally imposed racial blinders to see an essential person of another ethnic heritage.

My grandmother would have been pleased. I know I was.

At that time Lowell, a third-generation Japanese-American, and I, a haole, a white person of indeterminate European origins, had been married about four years. We'd moved from Iowa, my home state where we met, to Honolulu, Hawaii. We wanted our children to get to know their Nisei grandparents, Irene and Masao, and his six Sansei — third generation — brothers and sisters.

These new connections were rich and wonderful, and fraught with difficulties for all of us. I was one generation off an Iowa farm, reared in a smallish Midwestern city, with the attitudes and values inculcated by my white, Protestant, middle-class family. Lowell was Hawaii-born, reared by a Japanese mother who herself had been reared from infancy by an Hawaiian family named Waipa. Lowell was a lover of poi (ugh), raw fish (double-ugh) and all manner of things I had never seen before. He knew things I'd never dreamed of. His world was a vast expansion from my rural Iowa world. I loved and feared it.

Lowell and I seemed so different from each other then, and in Hawaii I was the stranger, the one who didn't know how to behave at a Buddhist funeral or even at an Uda family party.

I did my best. And somehow being married to Lowell and belonging to his family began opening my eyes to the diversity and beauty of the whole human family.

As a child I was taught that it wasn't polite to stare. If my gaze fell on a black person, my mom scolded me and took me away. And I could never ever ask that person questions, not in the friendliest of spirits.

And yet, if we cannot look at each other, we cannot connect. If we cannot speak, how can we become friends?

Of course the racial divides in our country are far more complex than this. But I changed. Learning to love my husband's face and everything about him taught me to look with acceptance at others, hoping they accepted me too.

I began to see individual faces, the shapes of eyes and ears and chins and mouths. What a wondrous array of people. It was at that stage that I saw the woman who resembled my grandmother.

Before long I began to pick out the distinctive characteristics of the Japanese, the Chinese, the Koreans and others. We are beautiful in our differences and our likenesses.

To me this is one powerful meaning of Genesis 1:27, NRSV:

So God created humankind in his image,
in the image of God he created them;
male and female he created them.

This passage and my own experience tell me that we are all God's family, every one of us made in the image of God.

Sophie in the Image

Sophie is three, going on four, a lovely red-headed, blue-eyed wonder. She always seems compact and perfect, as full of energy as a comet and with sparkling intelligence. When she was two, she talked and talked, but very softly so that at first I couldn't hear her and had no idea how much she had to say. Finally I bent my ear to listen carefully, and Sophie said a lot.

Even at her age, Sophie has opinions. She knows how things are supposed to be in her world, and makes her disgust known when they don't live up. Often it's just an expression on her rosy-cheeked face, or maybe it's tears, and sometimes, says her father, our son, it's with the full-fledged temper that reputedly comes with red hair. I have never personally seen this temper, but her father says it's impressive.

The most important thing about Sophie to me, aside from her being my adorable granddaughter, is that she seems so totally and completely herself. I've known only one other person who seems so much like that.

For years I've called my friend "an original," because I've never known anyone remotely like her. She is always exactly and completely who she is, no pretense, no artifice, no seeking to please or adopting different personas to suit the situation. She also has a kind of inner balance and harmony, a peacefulness within herself that shines out of her. Though I don't think she considers herself religious, somehow she has become, as I a Christian see her, wholly and perfectly the person God made her to be.

Sophie is my second encounter with such a person. In some significant way, Sophie simply IS. I know her parents are working to curb her temper, and she, like all children, needs the good upbringing she's getting, and many kinds of education. But temper and all, she seems to me, in a way I've never noticed in another child, already complete because she is so much herself.

This may be an illusion on my part, or maybe the wishful thinking of a grandmother, or a longing for the child in myself. But I peer into my mirror and see myself as so incomplete, so much of me still becoming. After decades of spiritual discipline and experience, I recognize myself as full of flaws and failings, with a core of insecurities that sometimes goes away but always returns. Often I feel barely adequate for the things God calls me to do.

And yet I too am who I am. Though I look with awe at the two "originals" in my life, Sophie and my friend, I, like all of us, am made in the image of God. Like everyone, I contain a core of divine beauty and completeness that flowers to perfection in God's love.

"So God created humankind in his image . . . male and female he created them." Genesis 1:27, NRSV. That includes Sophie, my friend and all of us.

Hide-and-seek

When I was a young girl in Iowa, one of my favorite games was hide-and-seek. I played with my friends in those long summer twilights as the fireflies came out and the light turned from gold to purple to deep, velvety blue.

I loved playing hide-and-seek. I'd squeeze myself into the most out-of-the-way places I could find, even risking spiders and other critters. Being found was a little disappointing, because I hadn't hidden well enough to fool my friends.

The only thing worse was not being found. Sometimes the other kids would lose interest and drift away, and there I'd be, crammed in some grotty place, still waiting for the sound of sneakers and giggles. Sometimes I hid too well and would have to crawl out covered with dirt and gunk while the other kids yelled at me.

At full dark, Mom would come out on the front stoop and holler for me. If I didn't hustle inside, pretty soon I'd hear my dad's ear-splitting whistle. He learned that whistle on the farm as a boy, and more than once he showed me how, but I never mastered it.

At that whistle, I'd really race. The next step was Dad coming to look for me, and I might get a swat on the rear. So I'd fly home, in and out of the shower, brush my teeth, jump into my pajamas and go kiss my parents good night. That was my world, safe, affectionate and mostly pre-dictable.

Douglas V. Steere, in *Dimensions of Prayer*, tells a Jewish Hasidic story about a rabbi's son who came home crying from playing hide-and-seek with his friends. The father asked the boy what had happened. "I hid," the boy said, "but nobody bothered to look for me."

The rabbi hugged his son and said that perhaps now the boy can understand know how God feels when he hides himself so that people will seek him. God is still waiting for them to come.

What a marvelous idea. God hides and wants us to seek him. God doesn't want us to decide that looking for him is too much trouble, or to be distracted from the search for him by the thousand other things that we have to do everyday. God wants to be found.

In the beginning, God was not hidden. God walked and talked with Adam and Eve in the Garden. In part the Old Testament is the story of how people, just like the First

Couple, couldn't seem to follow God's simple commands and God became more hidden.

The difference between the children's game of hide-and-seek and the way our God hides is that even hiding, God seeks us and never stops until we find him and put him at the center of our lives. When we do that, God no longer hides but is always present with us. I am reminded of my mom and dad in those long-ago times. They never failed to find me, even when my playmates ran away.

Debbie, Bride of Christ

She was the buzz at Sunday fellowship. Nobody said much to me, but I heard the questions. Who was she? Had she recently moved to our small town? Did she have family here? Was she crazy, wearing a get-up like that?

Debbie stood out from the crowd in her white sunbonnet and long white cotton dress with ruffles. She was quiet and soft-spoken, and introduced herself as the bride of Jesus Christ. Did I want to see her books?

That week I had two calls from people in neighboring towns. Debbie was dangerous and disruptive, they said. "She'll wreck your church," one warned. The other accused her of burning down her father's house. They wouldn't leave their names.

I don't place much credence in anonymous calls. By then I knew Debbie had been chased out of several other churches, but she too was God's beloved child. I was determined to make a place for her with us.

That week Debbie arrived at my study in her same white garb, lugging six enormous green books. They were filled with strange scrawls that I couldn't decipher and stick-figure drawings. She gave me one of her pictures that she said showed her wedding to Jesus. I put it on my bulletin board.

Still wearing her white dress and bonnet, she attended our services for six weeks, always quiet and pleasant. We welcomed her and found ways to help, with food from our church pantry and with housewares and furniture because her little trailer was almost empty.

Then one afternoon she visited me and wanted two hundred dollars for a bus trip to Texas to see a certain evangelist. I explained that my small pastor's fund was only for emergency needs such as baby formula and medicine.

"God told me to go," she insisted.

I explained again and she got furious, calling me evil and the devil. Several groups were meeting in our church right then, and I asked her to be quiet. She screamed louder, so I touched her elbow and walked her outside. Fortunately she came along easily, and at the door I asked her to return and visit me later. She only stared at me a moment and walked away.

In three weeks she returned to the church as if nothing had happened. She was still wearing her white bonnet and dress. No, she said when I asked her, she hadn't gone to Texas.

A few months later her trailer burned down and she moved away. I had a couple of letters from her and then they stopped. I missed her and I wasn't the only one. She had become part of us. After a year or so I took down her drawing of her "wedding to Jesus."

Who was Debbie? At the time I knew her as a beloved child of God who spent much of her time in a world very different from mine. Now I think maybe she was God's special angel, our messenger. In spite of our hesitations and insecurities, we welcomed her, and she taught us how to be more loving. God's angels come in all shapes and sizes, and they always bring great gifts.

Child of God

My father considered himself a hard-driving businessman. During WWII he served in the battlefields of Okinawa, and as I was growing up he taught me that our country does not wage aggressive wars against other nations the way Germany and Japan did.

My father also taught me about the Jesus of the Sermon on the Mount, that wonderful distillation of Christianity which is perhaps the greatest religious teaching ever. "You have heard it said, 'An eye for an eye and a tooth for a tooth.' But I say to you, Do not resist an evildoer. But if anyone strikes you on the right cheek, turn the other also...." Matt. 5:38. "[For] I say to you, Love your enemies and pray for those who persecute you...." Matt. 5:43.

Jesus taught truths that are extremely hard to live by. "Put your sword away," he said to Peter, after Peter cut off the ear of the high priest's servant, "for all who take the sword will perish by the sword." Matt. 26:52.

My dad carried a Bible throughout WWII, and read it faithfully. He believed that Jesus meant what he said about perishing by the sword, and all those other difficult truths, and he taught me to believe them too. Yet he went off to war.

He said, "War is terrible. I hate it. But I had to go." He loved his country with the passion of a farm boy who was at home with the black soil and lush greens of southeastern Iowa, and he showed me, in an Iowa cornfield in August, how you can hear the snap and crackle of the corn growing.

What Dad had most wanted to do with his life was to become a minister. But the Great Depression intervened and it was not to be.

Then, in wartime he did things that he thought were unforgivable, because at the time they seemed necessary. He said, "We used flame-throwers in caves that turned out to hold old people and children, even infants. It was as bad as Vietnam, but there weren't any media around."

Then he was dying, and I remember his tremulous voice when he asked, "Joanie, can God forgive me?"

I think he knew the answer and that his heart was full of repentance. And I said, "Yes. Absolutely." How could I be so sure?

Three days before he died, my father had a vision. He walked out of his bedroom, the last time he ever walked alone. He kept saying, over and over, "Can you see the colors? The colors are so beautiful." Then he told Helen and me, "I went somewhere, and I'm not supposed to talk about it. I've probably already said too much. But oh, the colors."

Some might argue that this was his painkillers at work, or maybe oxygen deprivation from the cancer that had moved into his lungs. But I don't think so. I believe God was easing Dad's burden and showering him with forgiveness. My dear father died knowing he was God's beloved child.

How to Be Really Special

My adoptive parents were wonderful. They cared deeply for me. To ease any psychological trauma I might have from being adopted, they taught me that I was special. "You're so special," they'd say, "that we went looking for you, and when we found you we couldn't wait to bring you home."

Many situations in life, though, are full of pitfalls. Even when we see the pitfalls clearly, we can't always avoid them. This was one of those.

Being special was a pit I fell into. My parents couldn't have guessed that I, in my childish way, would take being special as both an excuse for puffed-up pride and a burden. A need to be special has dogged me all my life until recently, and I'm not sure it's completely gone.

My heavens, why else would I need three professional degrees? Well, there's more to it than that. I do love education, and I have all these insecurities, but I see the tracks of my needing to be special through all my years of striving for A's and wanting to be at the top of my class. Most people get over that stuff in high school or college. I was "special" on steroids.

The other day I saw all of this clearly. I had just finished a time of Scripture reading, prayer and meditation. I had been asking God for weeks to show me the broken places in my spirit that remain invisible to me. I know they're there, because when I match who I am with who I think God wants me to be, I see great discrepancies.

My new understanding happened when I stepped into the shower. The hot water beat in my face, I was totally relaxed, and it came in a series of pictures or what you might call visions, in clear and colorful detail, myself at many stages of my life being so "special."

There it was, full blown and beautiful, containing new healing truths to mend more of my brokenness. Of course it was painful too, but the pain was only a flash, dispersed almost immediately by the knowledge that this would allow me to grow spiritually. In some subtle way this experience changed, and is still changing, my life.

It seems a miracle to me that God works this way, that God responds so directly to prayerful requests for self-understanding. In my experience this kind of prayer takes focus, repetition, and time, maybe even months. But, with perseverance, it always seems to come.

Knowing this once-hidden strand of my life doesn't mean I'll never need to feel special again. It does mean that I can pull back from old behaviors and find my specialness in the place God wants it: in relationship with God.

The fact is, the most special thing about me is that I,

like you and everyone else, am a beloved child of God, made in the image of God. I have finally come in my life to believe that nothing is more special than this.

Trailing Clouds of Glory

When I was ten my connection with God was still alive, though not as strong as when I was younger. In those days my prayers still felt vital and fresh, not as if they were dropping into a void. I felt close enough that if God ever decided to talk to me, I figured I'd recognize God's voice.

And then that feeling of closeness vanished. Like millions of my contemporaries growing up in the aftermath of WWII and during the Korean War, I actually turned away from God.

Perhaps this turning away had to do with a booming post-war economy, the surge in American consumerism, the huge upswing in my generation of children being sent to college, and the growing belief that science could solve all problems and God was now irrelevant.

Of course for every problem science has solved, more have been created, and happiness still doesn't lie in having a mini-mansion and three cars. I see so many people who once were happy, open-hearted children, and now want nothing to do with a life of faith. How grateful I am to be back.

Children are naturals in a relationship with God. While small, they are so unselfconscious, grace-filled without even trying. This must be one reason why Jesus said: "Truly I tell you, unless you change and become like children, you will never enter the kingdom of heaven." Matthew 18:3.

I remember a ten-year old girl in Colorado who announced to her parents and older sisters one day that she wanted to attend church. She didn't want to be dropped off for Sunday school as many children are. She wanted the whole family there. So her family visited several churches and allowed her to choose. Thus they became part of our church community.

The parents said they didn't know where she got the idea. She was the youngest child, and they didn't think she'd ever been to church before. It's amazing that she asked to come — and maybe even more amazing that the parents listened. It was a powerful thing to see them there, knowing their youngest child had brought them.

In thinking about this girl and her insistence on coming to church, I was reminded of a children's book I read decades ago when I was very young. I don't recall its title, but in it was a lively conversation between a baby and a robin that went something like this:

"So do you still see God?" Baby asked the robin.

"Yes," said the robin.

"I wish I could," Baby said. "I think I'm forgetting him."

The great English poet William Wordsworth must have understood this. In "Intimations of Immortality" he wrote:

Our birth is but a sleep and a forgetting:
The Soul that rises with us, our life's Star,
 Hath elsewhere its setting,
  And cometh from afar:
 Not in entire forgetfulness,
 And not in utter nakedness,
But trailing clouds of glory do we come
 From God, who is our home:
Heaven lies about us in our infancy!

Maybe we should consult all the babies we know. "Tell me again about God, Baby. I've almost forgotten."

FRUITS OF THE SPIRIT

4

The Fawn

I t was a little shock the first time I read, with adult comprehension, Galatians 5:22-23, which told me that "the fruit of the Spirit is love, joy, peace, patience, kindness, generosity, faithfulness, gentleness, and self-control." I was young and barely beginning my faith journey.

"This is lovely," I said to myself, "but it's not me. It's the me I'd like to be, but I don't know how."

I had no idea of the struggles and wonder that lay ahead. As a child I was often achingly introverted, fearful, and unable to explain myself even about simple things.

One of my most painful memories goes back to when I was about nine. My best friend was Ellen and we had a powerful bond because Ellen was also adopted. We used to pretend we were sisters, though I was less than two months older than she. We started school together, but by fourth grade, when this incident happened, I had moved with my parents to another school district.

I was at Ellen's house one summer afternoon on what we now call a play date. I remember vividly Ellen's immaculate small house and beautiful terraced back yard with big, mature elm trees. Ellen's mom called us inside for cookies and lemonade.

A newspaper with a photo of a fawn lay on the ottoman. Ellen's mom picked it up and showed it to us without comment. I glanced at it, didn't read the caption and thought the fawn was cute. I laughed. I saw only a real live Bambi lying there with its mama. I didn't realize that Ellen's mother was stifling horror at my reaction.

When my mom came to pick me up, she and Ellen's mother shooed us girls outside for a few minutes. We didn't mind. We loved being together.

Soon Mom and I left and when we were in the car headed home, Mom said, "Joan, why did you laugh at that photo? The fawn was dead!"

What? I hadn't seen blood or anything to suggest the fawn wasn't perfectly all right. I had completely misunderstood, and I felt humiliated. I also felt stupid, inadequate and unlovable, a fairly frequent state for me in those days.

"What must Erma be thinking?" my mom said. I tried to speak, to say, "I didn't know, I didn't get it," but the words clogged in my throat. I didn't really understand the reactions of the two moms, and I just wanted to disappear. I shrank into the car's upholstery, hoping Mom would wear out the subject soon.

In some important way I started that day to feel essentially invisible to the adults around me. It's a long, winding trail from where I was that summer afternoon to the person of love, joy, peace, patience, kindness, generosity, faithfulness, gentleness, and self-control that I wanted to be. Under my quiet, introverted exterior was a lot of anger. Anger doesn't allow much room for the fruits of the Spirit.

In those days I was so shy that I'd hang out by myself at recess, lonely and pretending I didn't care. When school let out I'd run home and sob. I felt ugly and dumb, a reject.

"Mommy," I'd cry, "nobody will play with me."

She'd say, "Just go up to them and ask if you can play."

Didn't she understand? They'd only laugh at me. Kids weren't any kinder then than they are now.

Dad said, "You always have to pretend you're not afraid. That's how you have to face every challenge."

At six-two a large-sized grown man, that was fine for him to say. It didn't occur to me that he'd once been young and small like me and that he'd come by his wisdom the hard way.

Eventually I listened and learned to quell my fears and

speak up, though often I couldn't quite say what I meant. Sometimes then frustration would cause my anger to come bursting out. I kept working on myself, and years later I went to law school, where I learned to be assertive and to discipline my anger.

Not long after law school I returned to the church. That was when I read the Galatians passage about the fruits of the Spirit. It set a whole new list of goals for my life. Only God knows if I'm a little closer these days, but I do know it's the most worthwhile journey I've ever taken. I'm convinced the best is yet to come.

Seize the Day

Every year my vision of the New Year is an unmarked expanse of new-fallen snow at night, sparkling under moonlight and stretching as far as the eye can see. A million stars twinkle overhead. It is a vast field of hope and possibility.

I suppose this image came from living most of my life in sparsely populated northern climates. It returns every year undimmed. About three days after Christmas my hope surges, and suddenly I'm dreaming about possibilities again.

My problem is, I've often found myself dragging a load of baggage from the old year into the new. Some of it is ancient, and I'll probably never know what happened.

~Fruits of the Spirit~

What I do know is that I grew up with a powerful fear of abandonment that I associate with the eleven weeks of my life before I was adopted by wonderful loving parents.

Some of it is newer, a load collected in a lifetime of being me. There's the dumb stuff I did as a teenager, some dopey decisions I made as a young parent, and a whole wagon full of the kind of pride that sometimes gets a person dumped on her head.

So I've been wondering if the idea of New Year's resolutions first sprang from someone's desire to unload some baggage permanently. I kind of stumbled into this notion because when I was in seminary I stopped making resolutions that sounded like "to do" lists. I had to dig for something deeper and, thanks to a friend, discovered a single resolution that I've held since then: "Stay close to God."

It was so simple, so easy to remember. Plus I wrote it in places where I couldn't avoid seeing it many times a day. The means were obvious: worship, prayer, meditation, study, interacting in a loving way with everyone. All the things that can get lost in the shuffle and bustle of daily life, even for pastors.

Amazingly — oh, that amazing grace again — change happened. During those years, my relationship with God strengthened and deepened, the relationship which for Christians is the model for all other relationships. Lots of baggage fell off my wagon, so to speak. I found myself striving less and "just being" more, and all those fruits of the Spirit that the Apostle Paul lists in Galatians 5:22-23, love, joy, peace, patience, kindness, generosity, faithfulness, gentleness and self-control, didn't seem nearly so far out of my reach.

So this year, as the old year turns into the new, I'm recommitting to the old resolution, and adding one more: carpe diem. Seize the day. My recent surgery taught me a lot of things. Staying close to God is the most important, but right up there is living each day to the fullest. Being human, I know my days are numbered. I want to live each one to the max, close to God and with a loving heart that rejects boundaries and reaches out to everyone.

Here's to a happy and blessed New Year.

Abiding Grace

Years ago a local law enforcement officer told me about working as an urban police officer, in an area where even cops get nervous. One night he saw a bunch of people hanging around a bonfire in an alley. They watched as he approached, and suddenly a man pulled a handgun and fired three times at my friend almost point blank. Each time the gun misfired.

~Fruits of the Spirit~

My friend said, "I was a goner. I knew it, he knew it. Instantly my whole life passed in front of me. And boy, I didn't like what I saw. Then I found myself still alive. I knew it was time to change."

I find my friend's response marvelous: he turned his life around. Many people after a brush with death would celebrate their good luck and that would be the end of it. Others might think of changing their lives, but old habits die hard, so after a few fits and starts, not much happens.

My friend never told me the details of his transformation, but when I met him years later he was a genuinely good guy with a great sense of humor, and he'd become an active church member.

I need to be clear: I don't think Jesus stuck a finger into the muzzle of that gun to save my friend's life. If I did, then what could I say about all the times the gun fires and good people die?

But I'm convinced God's grace was waiting for my friend in that dark alley, as it waits for all of us everywhere. Grace waited for me for years as I proudly rebelled against "religion," by which I meant the church of my childhood that I experienced as stuffy and autocratic.

Grace waited for me until one of the darkest nights in my life, when I simply had to face that I'd made a mess of things. I could hardly remember how to pray, so I only mumbled, "Okay, I can't do this anymore. It's in your hands." It's hard for me to admit that I was sobbing.

In that moment God forgave my puny self-centeredness, and wrapped me in a blaze of light that seemed as big, beautiful and limitless as the universe. That was the beginning of grace's transformative power in me, a power that is still at work.

God's grace is free — we can't earn it, we just have to receive it. The thing is, once grace enters us, it begins reshaping our lives. Soon we want to pass it on by doing God's work in the world. That's how we know it's the real thing. Increasingly grace inspires who we are becoming and how we live and behave.

This is one reason we call grace amazing. It reaches into dark alleys, bedrooms and all kinds of places to find and embrace us. Then, if we welcome it, grace abides with us throughout our lives, giving us frequent glimpses of the incredible light that is God.

Practicing Faith

My friend was searching for a spiritual life. One day she told me, "I tried going to church, but it didn't do a thing for me, so I didn't go back."

I told her I understood. When I moved away from my

parents' home, I left the church. It seemed so remote, antiquated and dull. It didn't seem to relate to my life.

Twenty years later when my mother unexpectedly died, I started hearing old hymns in my head: "Amazing Grace," "Tell Me the Stories of Jesus," "Holy, Holy, Holy!" Somehow they called me to look at myself and helped me to see how low the embers of my spirit had burned.

I tried to pray, but couldn't remember how. I had a narrow and stultifying idea of what prayer is. Finally I seized on a line from a hymn: "Open my heart." I prayed it many times a day, for weeks.

During that time, I started going to church. It felt so strange. The hymns were different and I didn't know anybody. I persisted because my spiritual hunger was huge.

Eventually, over a period of years, I found my way back to a faith that was much like the faith of my childhood, simple and trusting. It grew slowly as bit by bit I received God back into my heart.

I discovered that a lively spiritual life doesn't happen just by wanting it or in isolation. It takes community and spiritual discipline. God doesn't drag us into faith. We have to present ourselves and seek.

So I told my friend to try a few churches, pick the one that felt most comfortable and keep going until she felt something kindling in her soul. I found church the best place to encounter God, though now those encounters happen for me almost everywhere, including church. Church makes a quiet space in life to rest the mind, let the holy in and feel God's presence and peace.

Eventually I found my own place in a church community, and I was sure she would too. I told her to look for the wonderful people, the ones who have opened their minds and hearts to God and do their best to live the life faith teaches. They are often quiet and unassuming, not always the visible leaders. They are always there, though, because no church can survive without them.

In 1738 John Wesley, founder of Methodism, encountered one of these wonderful people. Wesley was a young Anglican clergyman struggling because his faith lacked conviction. He confessed his problem to Peter Böhler, a Moravian church leader. Böhler counseled, "Preach faith till you have it; and then because you have it you will preach faith."

What I suggested to my friend was similar. "Practice faith until you have it. Then because you have it, share it and your journey will grow and thrive."

This approach is why we have spiritual communities and disciplines. It works for great spiritual leaders, and even for ordinary pilgrims like me.

Talking to Myself

In the '80s, a psychologist named Jerome Brunner studied two-year-old Emily, whose parents observed that Emily talked to herself every night in her crib before she snuggled down to sleep. They tape-recorded tiny Emily, making 122 transcripts in 15 months.

Brunner's team of linguists and psychologists scrutinized these transcripts, discovering that Emily's bedtime self-talk was far more complicated, in everything from ideas to grammar, than the way she talked to her parents.

Brunner realized that little Emily was telling fairly elaborate stories about her days and the things she wanted or expected to happen: "And then Carl [her friend] and Emily are both going down the car with somebody, and we're going to ride to nursery school [whispered], and then…we're all going to get out of the car, go into nursery school, and Daddy's going to give us kisses…then he's going to work and we're going to play at nursery school. Won't that be funny?"

I don't think Emily is unique. I remember hearing my own toddlers do this, though I didn't pay enough attention. Recently I've heard my young grandchildren doing it. It is, I believe, a spectacularly important kind of meaning-making, a child constructing the world he or she will live in.

I think this world-constructing continues through life, though many of us, including yours truly, are minimally aware that we do it. Teenagers talk relentlessly on the phone. In the days of one home line, it was, "Suzie, get off the phone; your dad has to make a call." Now it's cell phones glued to our ears.

I remember the days of long coffee-klatches with other young mothers, spinning endless tales of husbands and children. Even now I like to get on the phone with my daughters, telling stories that continue to entwine our lives. And think of books, magazines, newspapers, TV and radio. Huge flows of world-constructing words for those who write, speak and hear them.

The problem is, sometimes our meaning-making words are hurtful or dysfunctional. One of the hardest things for me to learn about life and being a religious person — I'm still working on this — is that in most ways I am author of my own life. I write my autobiography in deeds and words, and I'm the one responsible for it. And I'm the only one with the author-ity to change the parts I don't like.

I had to wrestle in seminary with this idea of authority. Later I had to claim it in the pulpit. I'm the author of my own life, and sometimes it's difficult to write a good, caring story.

That's why I made a conscious choice to link my story

to that of a God who loves me so much that God became human to show me how to live and how to die. This eternal God-story keeps me going in the right direction. Some days it isn't easy, and there are other great stories. But for me this is the one that offers true happiness.

Gratitude

As Thanksgiving approaches, I can hear in my head that old hymn, "Come, ye thankful people, come, raise the song of harvest home." Thanksgiving is a wonderful season, and I am so happy. Last January I learned that I had a serious heart condition and needed major surgery. We found a skilled surgeon and now I'm recovering, and relearning the sheer delight of being alive. My heart overflows with gratitude.

When I discovered how bad my condition was, I had a quiet chat with God. Essentially God said, "Don't worry, all is well. You're going to learn a lot."

"Hmmm," I said to myself. "I'm not sure I like the sound of that." When God says I'm going to learn a lot, it's usually a lesson I'd rather avoid or put off.

But then God did for me what I believe God is always trying to do for all of us. God wrapped me in an astonishing, almost unbelievable peace. I didn't expect it, and at the time I simply floated in it, without realizing how life-giving and complete it was. Talk about amazing grace.

I'm thankful for so much this past year: for my terrific family physician, my skilled surgeon, Boom-Boom in intensive care, and all the other great medical personnel; for my loving and attentive family; and for my life itself.

And now I understand that this giving thanks is a way sweeter deal than I ever realized. It's far more than a quick mumble before passing the turkey, more than the delicious stuffing and the beloved faces gathered around the table.

Feeling gratitude, I've found, is also a powerful force for personal health and happiness. In recent years we've heard a lot about the toll stress takes on our minds and bodies, through its deadly relationship to heart disease, cancers and all kinds of emotional miseries.

But now we're learning that one big key to stress reduction is feeling gratitude. It seems so simple. According to stress researcher Hans Seyle, gratitude has a huge effect on "our peace of mind, our feelings of security or insecurity, of fulfillment or frustration, in short the extent to which we can make a success of life."

Wow. All of that. I think God must have worked it out. If we count our blessings, feel grateful for each and every one, and tell God about it — God who already knows but offers us the benefits of telling — our pulse rates slow, our blood pressures drop, our stress drains away, our anger or upset fizzles, and that opens us up to those wonderful feelings of joy, peace and contentment. Best of all, we come closer to God.

How perfect for Thanksgiving Day. How perfect for every day. When I look at you, I'll thank God for you. When you look at me, please do likewise — even if I am occasionally a small pain. How simple. How healing. God bless and Happy Thanksgiving.

Spiritual Security

Several years ago in another state, a security salesman phoned. He plunged directly into his spiel, explaining that nowadays I'm right to be frightened, it's a dangerous world, but if I would just purchase one of his home security systems, my worry would be over.

I tried to be polite. "No thanks, I'm not in the market for a security system."

"Just let me show you. These are great systems. You can't be too careful. Haven't you heard about the recent burglaries in your neighborhood?"

I had, but sometimes I get ornery. I attribute this to the residual lawyer in me. "I'm a pastor, so I'm in a different security business," I said. "My real security comes from

God."

I heard a deep breath, then click. He didn't even say goodbye. I'd become a bad prospect.

But ornery or not, I was telling him the truth. There comes a time in a growing faith life that old fears and insecurities start shifting. The oldest, really hard-core childhood ones begin revealing themselves, and once they're known, they're usually manageable or can be worked with. Others simply disappear.

I don't deny that the world can be a scary place. Even small towns in Montana aren't always safe. I remember years ago when I emerged from my downtown law office after midnight to see blood stains on the Last Chance Gulch sidewalk. I never learned what happened that night. I guessed that a fight had spilled out from a nearby bar. And we've all seen the white crosses that dot our landscape, mute testimony to untimely deaths along our highways. Substances are in our water, air and soil that most of us can hardly stand to think about. As the theme song for TV detective Monk says, "It's a jungle out there." You don't have to be obsessive-compulsive like Monk to know the dangers.

And yet God reigns. Deeply religious people and poets know there is a stillness at the center of things, utter peace, what the Buddhists call emptiness. Where all the gibbering inner voices cease, whether about bills, my sticky kitchen floor or my next medical checkup.

In the many years I traveled from lawyer to pastor, I learned that finding that still center takes time and spiritual discipline, including the willingness to face my own fears and let them overwhelm me, if that's what they need to do. I discovered that I have to be willing to shed tears and to accept myself as a sinner — one who frequently forgets to behave as God wishes — and that I can't remain long in the still center.

Eventually the journey brought me to a whole new kind of security. In this security a loving, forgiving God is ever present and Jesus Christ stands with me through everything. A bad traffic moment can frighten me, but I don't live on a tightrope of fear, waiting to fall or wondering what's gaining on me. God's security equals freedom. I highly recommend it.

Holy Humor

Tomorrow is Holy Humor Sunday in my husband's church. The Sunday after Easter is the day to laugh and let mirth take wing. Remember Abraham and Sarah? When God told Abraham that he and childless Sarah would have a son, Abraham fell down and laughed, and said to himself,

"Can a child be born to a man who is a hundred years old? Can Sarah, who is ninety years old, bear a child?" Sarah, hearing the news, also laughed.

God was not offended by their laughter. In fact God named their son Isaac, which means laughter.

I think God rejoices to see us laughing and happy, the way we are when we're good to each other and others are good to us. Proverbs 17:22 tells us that a cheerful heart is good medicine. Laughter cures the blues, and helps to heal mind, spirit and body. Ever tried to stay angry or feel down when laughing? I can vouch: it doesn't work.

Leonard Sweet, author and professor, gives us the "Jesus Code for Healthful Living." A few examples: laugh a lot; fullness of joy is the infallible sign of the presence of God. Also, hang out with friends, because God redeems us through relationships. Good friends teach us who we are and help us become whole. And don't forget to play out the child in you; we can only grow spiritually when we're curious, vulnerable and loving.

Once I read a study that said small children laugh dozens of times a day, adults not much more than ten. That tells us something — maybe that we're often too serious. Adult life sobers us right up. Last Monday we filed our tax return and I was Mrs. Grumpy by the time I was done with it. Most days heart disease isn't a huge chuckle either.

Ecclesiastes says, "For everything there is a season, and a time for every matter under heaven," including a time to weep and a time to laugh. Evidently knowing I needed to find more time to laugh, friends not long ago gave me a book called How to Keep Laughing — Even Though You've Considered All the Facts. I chortled my way through it.

G.K Chesterton once observed, "Life is serious all the time, but living cannot be. You may have all the solemnity you wish in your neckties, but in anything important (such as sex, death and religion), you must have mirth or you will have madness."

I loved that H.L. Mencken, one of America's great iconoclastic newspapermen, once defined Puritanism as "the lurking fear that somewhere someone may be having fun." I am no Puritan. On the other hand, I am a Methodist, of whom he wrote that if you're in a cold room, sit next to a Methodist, because they give off more heat.

Christ has risen, spring is in the air, so let's enjoy all the good laughs we can.

And the heavenly choir sang: Amen to that.

Frazzle and Dread

I sweated. I fretted. I had visions of Homeland Security smacking me, my medications and my metal hip up against the wall, saying, "You'll never fly again." I even prayed, asking to be relieved of this crazy dread that rose as I prepared to fly to Virginia to visit my daughter and her family.

I hadn't flown for four years, and the regulations about carry-ons have become much more complicated. As I studied them, my dread grew. I needed to carry on liquids, creams and gels, medications I couldn't risk losing.

My gracious son-in-law called the airline to double check how to pack things. He was shuttled to someone in India who said that all medications, including pills, must be carried on in their original bottles, jars or tubes, with pharmacy labels attached showing doctor, prescription number, and my name.

Oh, great. I hadn't really panicked until I heard this. Me with my titanium hip, chest repaired with stainless-steel bailing wire and all these medications, going through security? Would I be allowed to fly?

A friend advised, "Take only the pills you need, but in their original bottles."

"They're so big," I wailed. Huge bottles that come with a layer of tiny pills on the bottom. I don't get why they use such big bottles. Take all those?

Dutifully I dumped each type of pill into a plastic sandwich bag, counted out enough for my trip and put those back in the bottle. I packed my computer with layers of pill bottles, worrying all week long.

Several times it crossed my mind that I didn't really have to take this trip. My family would forgive me if I chickened out.

The day arrived. At the airport by 5:45 a.m. Checked in by 6 a.m. Then, frazzled, on to security. The very fulcrum of dread.

My hip and baling wire did not set off the alarm. Nobody seemed to look at my pills. They barely glanced at how I'd packed my gels, liquids and creams. When I was on the other side, having received nothing but cheerful good will, I waved to my husband and got teary. A kindly guard handed me a wad of tissues.

So much for all my fears. As I walked toward my gate, I was appalled at that frightened, timid me, the same person who used to love to fly and oozed self-confidence.

I received a huge lesson that day in the power of irrational fear. Over pill bottles and going through security? I faced open heart surgery with virtually no fear. What was this about?

The human propensity to fear still runs deep and wide in me, popping up when I least expect it. No matter how I love and trust God, these pockets of fear remain. I am imperfect in trust as I am imperfect in love.

The remarkable thing is that when I stumble God forgives and picks me up. When I face my fear, God strengthens me. It's grace, pure and simple.

THE POLITICAL
IS SPIRITUAL

5

Door to Door

Some years ago I ran for district judge. I was a lawyer in those days, and I ran twice. My issue was fairness for all who come before the courts. The judges I knew were mostly fair, but I'd seen firsthand that the system was weighted in favor of status, power and affluence. I wanted to see if I could "level the playing field," a sports metaphor used in many civil rights cases that provided justice for the less favored.

The first time I ran, it was five months, from January to early June, of excitement and hard work. I was disappointed when I ranked third in the nonpartisan primary with six other candidates.

I wasn't discouraged by this defeat, though, and I ran again in four years. I worked almost nonstop on my campaign, going door-to-door every afternoon from about four-fifteen to eight o'clock. The great part of my door-to-door was meeting many wonderful people and seeing much of Helena, the town I love so dearly and have lived in for so long, on foot.

I also had more than a few close encounters with dogs.

To communicate friendliness with dogs, I've learned, you talk to them in a high-pitched tone suggesting, "I'm not a threat. Let's play." Only one dog, I recall, did not respond to this approach with great waggings of tails and doggie smiles. Fortunately he was inside a fence. I did not open that gate.

I won in the primary but lost in the November general election. For a month or two I was crushed.

What I didn't realize at the time was that I was beginning a new and different journey. A little over a year after that election, my husband started looking at seminaries and talking about where to enroll. It's not so much that he experienced a call to ministry as that he decided to listen to the call that had been waiting for him since his youth.

I closed my law practice and off we went to Denver.

There I worked in law for a couple of years, until God broke through my own reluctance to hear my call. The year after Lowell was graduated from the Iliff School of Theology, I signed on.

~The Political Is Spiritual~

Talk about a kid in a candy store. I loved the school, the classes, the faculty and the students. I just couldn't get enough.

Then out I went to pastor churches, another thrilling and soul-fulfilling time.

I have been blessed in my journeying, my on-going search for God, who has always been on the journey with me. It's only in looking back that I notice how often this journey has asked me to move on, in both large and small ways.

I admire those who travel with less commotion, and those who can stay in one physical setting and yet know the world. I'm reminded of the poet Emily Dickenson whose travels seem so limited and whose poems capture so much that's important in life.

I never saw a moor,
I never saw the sea;
Yet know I how the heather looks,
And what a wave must be.

I never spoke with God,
Nor visited in heaven;
Yet certain am I of the spot
As if the chart were given.

~At the Water's Edge~

I wish I had Dickinson's gifts, but this is not me. I'm the person who comes to a place, explores it as deeply as I'm able, and then hears a call to move on. I go, though often reluctantly. This has been my life since I was a child.

This pattern might have begun in my infancy, when I was first given up by my birth mother and then adopted. Or maybe it started when my dad was called up during WWII and moved Mom and me from Cedar Rapids, Iowa, to Riverside, California, to Galveston, Texas, to Long Island, New York, and then to Iowa City, Iowa.

Or possibly that early experience meshed with an often restless personality that thus is willing to hear God's calls to move on.

What I've learned on my journey is that the closer I feel to God, the less what we usually call politics means to me. I am impatient with party politics of any persuasion. I long to see people acting in a Godly way, taking their cues from the Jesus of the Gospels.

I don't mean talking a good line. I mean living out the Sermon on the Mount. I want to see the Beatitudes functioning in Congressional votes and Presidential policies.

As I've lost interest in political parties and electoral politics — though I do vote regularly — I've come more and more to see that my political behavior needs to be a direct expression of my spirituality.

~The Political Is Spiritual~

If I say I believe Jesus when he says, "If anyone strikes you on the cheek, offer the other also," Luke 6:29, then how does this affect my attitudes about war? Don't I have to question a doctrine of "preemptive strike"? Don't I have a Christian duty to question any warlike acts by anybody, instead of rushing to a position of striking back?

If I say I believe Jesus when he says, "Feed my sheep," John 21:15, then what duty do I have to the millions of people who go hungry every day of their lives? I know I can't help them all, so what would Jesus have me do?

God looks directly into my heart and sees my deepest self. God sees not only what I do but why I do it. The wonderful thing is that God always understands and is ready to help me when I need to do better.

For me, "political" has to do with our lives in community. The tiniest part of it is partisan politics. The important part is how I live my life. It's about how I treat the other people on my block and across the world. It's whether I recycle cans, newspapers and batteries. It's about composting, growing food and creating loveliness with flowers.

By our fruits we are known. Matthew 7:20. In this sense, everything we do is political.

Kindergarten Rules

My five-year-old granddaughter recently had her kindergarten physical. She had three shots and a finger poke. As she left, she informed the nurse, "I'm not happy. I have one — no, two — no, three things I'm not happy about. I'm not angry, but I'm not happy."

I asked my daughter if the nurse reacted. "Not really," my daughter said, "she just stood there."

Based on the nurses I've known, she was thinking plenty. What a funny little kid, maybe. Or, Mom will have her hands full with that one in another ten years. Or something like my daughter's comment, "I think it's good that she's learning to say what she thinks."

So do I. I'm glad my granddaughter is learning to know what she feels and to put it into words. I'm reminded of my elder grandson who was known in grade school as a peacemaker. When another boy knocked him down on the playground, he stood up, said to the other boy, "That was not nice," and that ended it. The teacher told his mother, my other daughter, "I so appreciate your son. He has a real gift. I can put him in a bunch of rowdy kids, and everybody settles down." This year he turns 17, and to all reports he still has this gift.

This childhood moral clarity and willingness to speak

up is, I think, one of the many reasons Jesus said, "Truly I tell you, unless you change and become like children, you will never enter the kingdom of heaven." Matt. 18:3.

When I deconstruct what my granddaughter said, it's clear to me that she understands and probably agrees with the purpose of the shots and finger poke. If she thought it out, she might say, "Yes, Mom says these will help keep me well and take care of me, so that must be right, but it hurts and I'm not happy." For her own greater good, she knows she must put up with some unpleasantness. But there's no point in having a tantrum over it, though it's okay to be unhappy for a while.

Pretty sophisticated for a five-year-old. Such moral clarity might seem surprising in one so young. But I've seen her on a playground being equally clear. She hopped up on the play structure with children she didn't know, and was friendly and cooperative. But when another child tried to bump her off the top after she'd just climbed up, she said politely, "Just a second; it's my turn now."

Jesus came to teach us our kindergarten rules. Don't push or try to grab somebody else's lunch money. Take turns. Share. Be kind. Don't bite, spit or kick. Treat everybody the way you wish to be treated.

Simple rules, though we grownups do seem to complicate them. I'm clear, though, that they're the gateway to

God's great kingdom, which, Jesus says, is already among us, and yet, paradoxically and wonderfully, is also still on the way.

God's Politics

Jim Wallis's book, *God's Politics*, is subtitled *Why the Right Gets It Wrong and the Left Doesn't Get It*. He explains that no matter what anybody says, God is not a Republican or Democrat. God's politics are real, and all about how we treat each other here on earth. God's politics critique both parties.

Wallis calls himself a progressive evangelical. He founded and has maintained the Gospel-based Sojourner's Magazine, the social action group Call to Renewal and various social programs in Washington, D.C.

Even knowing Wallis's powerful commitments, I was shocked to read his quote from James Forbes, pastor of Riverside Church in New York City: "Nobody gets to heaven without a letter of reference from the poor!"

Wow! I didn't want to hear that. I'd never seen it put so starkly. It reminded me of Matthew's parable about the rich young man who asked Jesus how to gain eternal life. Jesus replied: "Go, sell your possessions, and give the money to the poor. . . ."

~The Political Is Spiritual~

What a huge challenge. I've wrestled with it for years, starting when I began taking God seriously in my own life.

Logically, says my brain, if I sell my possessions and give the money to the poor, then I am the poor. It's terrifying. I've stood with the homeless and hopeless — I've served meals to them, lobbied for them, given money for them. And God forgive me, I don't want to join them. Considering the state of my health, I doubt I'd last a year.

The fact is, I'm among the unjustly privileged of the world. It's not because I'm more deserving, smarter or better looking than our brothers and sisters out there who worry about where their next meal is coming from. If you know me, you know I'm not so deserving, smart or attractive.

It's because, solely, that I was raised by a middle-class American family, taught the value of education, and enjoyed very good health until recently. I had plenty of opportunities and seized all I could. It's true that I've worked hard all my life, but I didn't create the opportunities and privilege myself. I was born into them. And accepted them for my first twenty-five years as merely how things are.

But I'm weary of how things are. In my newly mended heart is a vision of how we can all live together governed by God's justice and peace, where no child goes to bed hungry and no older person suffers from loneliness or inadequate medical attention. Where dreamers dream and leaders are willing to hear the truth, and war becomes the last resort.

I think any steps toward these things are letters of reference from the poor. We have only to raise our voices and insist on the kind of country, the kind of world we want, where justice is for everybody and kindness rules our lives. We have only to adopt God's politics in both public and private life, in words, deeds and funds.

Family Migrations

My dad once told me, "Grandpa Moehle was a farmer back in Germany, and he came to the States with nothing but a shovel and a hoe. He came to escape conscription into the Prussian army and to find his own land." Grandpa Moehle settled near Burlington, Iowa, hired out as a farm hand, saved his pennies and eventually started buying farmland.

"When I was little," Dad said, "Grandpa took me out in his fields and told me, 'Varren, first you put your foot on dis piece of land,' stamping his right foot down, 'and den you put your foot on anodder piece of land,' stamping his left." According to Dad, Grandpa Moehle believed that owning land was the path to safety, enough to eat, and the freedom to mind his own business.

~The Political Is Spiritual~

On the McAllister side of the family, the records go back to Alexander McAllister, born October 10, 1749, near Edinburgh, Scotland, and died February 9, 1826, at Halifax, Pennsylvania. Alexander's wife Elizabeth made it to Burlington, Iowa, where she died in 1853. Dad never said much about his McAllister ancestors, except that he was one-quarter Scots and the rest was German.

These were people on the move, like Dad and me. Dad loved the rich Iowa farmland, yet he traveled the globe as a soldier, and then later, with my mother, as a tourist. He died in Napa, California, in 1991.

As for me, I've lived in Iowa, Illinois, New York, Texas, California, Hawaii, Colorado and Montana, and have traveled outside the U.S.

What is all this motion, this perpetual movement? We give lots of reasons, but my guess is, there's also something hardwired into us that pushes us to pick up and go. Our human story is about migration.

Maybe the first big migration happened when our earliest ancestors left Africa for other parts of the world, or so the anthropologists suggest. Another was when native Asians migrated across what is now the Bering Strait into the Americas. Staid old Europe was a regular hotbed of migration, with Gauls, Celts, Mongols and Muslims pushing out in different directions. Eventually Europeans migrated to the Americas, to find "indigenous Americans" already here. Everybody, it seems to me, has been on the move forever.

Can we stop this human tide, even with mile-high walls? Remember the Great Wall of China? The Berlin Wall?

So how should a religious person respond when we find newcomers among us? Deuteronomy 10:19 says, in a longer version of the Ten Commandments: "...love the stranger, for you were strangers in Egypt." Jesus says: "I was a stranger and you welcomed me." Matthew 25:35. Welcoming the stranger, he makes clear, is an essential key to heaven. We humans are not heaven's gatekeepers. Jesus is both the gate and its keeper.

We all at times have to be the stranger. I am so glad that America welcomed my ancestors, and eventually my husband's from Asia, and in so doing, welcomed me and my whole family.

Polar Bears

Polar bears have always sparked my imagination, touching something wild and sheerly incredible in myself.

They are the largest land carnivores, yet so full of flowing grace, even under water as I've experienced them at the

Denver zoo. They are marvelous to behold even in captivity. Smaller polar bears weigh around 800 pounds, and the big ones can be over 1400 pounds and up to nine feet long. That's a lot of graceful bear.

In the wild polar bears live in what seems like a most inhospitable place. They spend most of every year on the great ice floes up north, hunting seals, walruses, narwhales and fish. When the ice melts in summer, they return to land, but on land they have no prey, and so must fast until the great freeze in the fall.

I'm moved by their incredible power, their endurance, and their ability to become such tender and loving mothers. Pictures of mothers and young bears just seem to radiate affection.

Maybe this is why news that polar bears are in trouble is so disturbing to me. The arctic ice is melting, so the bears' hunting season is getting shorter and their fasting time on land is longer. Scientists are finding bears with inadequate body fat, and babies are being born at lower birth weights. As the ice melts, the bears have a harder time hunting and sometimes drown because the ice becomes too thin to support them.

Saddest of all, it seems that hungry polar bears are now turning to cannibalism. Adult males are starting to kill and eat nursing females and juvenile bears.

~At the Water's Edge~

The Denver polar bear exhibit had great slabs of rock for the bears to lie on, and deep pools with glass fronts so we humans could see them under water.

One bear, though, who looked old and world-weary to me, endlessly head-butted the door to outside. He'd back up a few feet and just keep butting. Every time I visited the zoo, he was still charging that door. Maybe he thought it was the way back to that great arctic wilderness where polar bears roam free, raise families, live and die on the huge expanses of ice.

Scientists say that polar bears may go extinct in 100 years. They may die out in my grandchildren's lifetimes.

Should it matter? Soul to soul, I related to that head-butting bear. If I were in his place, I'd be butting that door too.

God made polar bears as God made you and me. God gave us humans dominion over everything on earth, by which I understand that we are charged with stewardship of the whole creation. We are, I believe, accountable for all living things, at least to the extent that our conduct affects them.

I also think these wonderful animals help to define who we are. We relate to their wildness, their magnificence, their strangeness, and we know ourselves better in relation to them. When they become extinct, our world contracts.

And we ourselves are diminished.

The Luxury of Moral Judgments

What a luxury it is, I realized recently, to make moral judgments on anyone outside myself. It is also, I believe now, immoral.

When I am safe, have a home and plenty of food, with family and friends nearby, I have the basics and a lot more. I can sit in my comfortable living room or my car and fume, or listen to radio or TV commentators fulminating, about some hapless group. A few years ago it was people on welfare. These days it's immigrants. I am not in the shoes of those about whom I'm fuming.

And that's the rub. My Grandma Carlton taught me, "Don't judge until you've walked a mile in the other person's moccasins." My grandma was probably a better person than I'll ever be, and many of her teachings have stayed with me. It's possible I understood this better when I was twelve than in recent years.

But maybe now I'm getting it again. How easy it is, and how cruel, to judge others while having no experience of their practical circumstances.

I think of a Mexican laborer willing to risk death in a scorching desert because if he makes it to safety here without getting caught, he can earn enough to send a little money home to his hungry family every payday. He also becomes an illegal immigrant.

Here's the hard truth. The God I worship will always prefer a child with a full stomach to any arbitrary political boundary in the world.

I say "arbitrary" because political boundaries are not drawn on the earth. I remember the early astronauts sending home photos of our exquisitely lovely planet, and noting how there were no lines drawn on it separating nations or states. Boundaries are drawn on maps, because of wars or other kinds of conquest.

I'm aware of the complexities of immigration, and welfare too, for that matter. For every point of view, there is an equally strong, countervailing point of view.

But those of us who take our religion seriously are constrained by what our religion teaches.

"When you reap the harvest of your land," says Leviticus 19:9-10, "you shall not reap to the very edges of your field, or gather the gleanings of your harvest. You shall not strip your vineyard bare, or gather the fallen grapes of your vineyard; you shall leave them for the poor and the alien: I am the LORD your God."

Jesus, on his first visit to his hometown after the start of his ministry, says that the Lord has anointed him "to bring good news to the poor." Luke 4:16.

Care of the poor is one of the Five Pillars of Islam, and a requirement of the Compassionate Buddha.

My point is that if I want to call myself a religious person, I must filter my judgments through what my faith requires of me. If I don't or fail to act on it, I am behaving immorally according to the One I claim to follow.

The First Step

October is Domestic Violence Awareness Month. Thinking about domestic violence reminded me of my early marriage which ended about forty-five years ago. Funny how some misery is so hard to forget.

I married very young. My husband was four years older than I, and I thought he was terribly mature. I ignored my parents when they counseled me against marrying him. It was as if I couldn't even hear their voices.

When my parents visited, I'd explain my black eye by saying I walked into a door. Or that my bruises were caused by accidentally falling down the stairs.

I'm sure I was very angry at him, but somehow I buried that anger and spent a lot of time apologizing and trying to figure out how to do things right. I blamed myself.

I fibbed a lot to my parents, who lived in another state. They were not easy to fool, though, and one day my dad showed up at my door moments after my husband went to work. He said, "This is it, Joan. Grab the kids and the bare necessities, and let's go. Or we wash our hands of it."

I just stared at him for a minute, then I bundled up the children and fled.

My husband had threatened to kill all of us, so my dad drove us to my grandmother's house in another town. We hid out there for about three months, until the threats and nasty mail to my parents' house almost stopped. Then Dad took us home to his and Mom's house for a few more months.

In those days domestic shelters didn't exist. When I went looking for help outside the family, I didn't find any. I saw a lawyer, who told me he'd known my husband since high school and called me a liar. I was discouraged and almost gave up. Then, mercifully, my father appeared.

The rest of the story, of course, is that those were difficult years, though my parents continued to stand by me. Being a single parent demanded everything I had and more. I struggled with parenting, jobs and school. I set a pattern in those days of working myself to exhaustion, which probably wasn't smart but seemed necessary.

We survived and eventually the children thrived. I'm guessing my parents saved my life and maybe all of our lives. What grace they showed us, what courage and utter and unconditional love.

Did God have a hand in all this? I believe so. My parents' faith, love and courage, which were strengthened by their lifelong religious values and practice, gave me the faith, love and courage to carry on.

Many women in domestic abuse situations don't have such loving, courageous and motivating family members. But today all over the country there are good, safe, compassionate shelters that offer refuge and much more to anyone escaping abuse. These are wonderful havens for women and children and sometimes even men who are in need. God bless all of the shelters everywhere, and all the terrific people who work so hard to make them possible.

A Resolution for All of Us

As the New Year approaches, I'm thinking that our communities need a special New Year's resolution.

I was shocked that four homeless people died this year in the Montana town where I live, though hundreds, probably thousands, died throughout our country. A newspaper editorial on Dec. 24 quoted a survey from January 2006 finding 2,311 homeless people in this sparsely populated state. Our homeless included infants, children, older people, and even some Korean War veterans. Many of the adults hold jobs but don't earn enough to rent a place and still afford to eat.

It's shameful. In "the land of the free and the home of the brave," how free and brave are we if we cannot face the truth of homelessness in our community? In our land of plenty, why is it that we, as a society, don't share our plenty in more meaningful ways?

I don't mean to suggest that none of us help. Clearly we do, and many of us give as much money and time as we can, and sometimes more. It just isn't enough.

I try to picture myself having to sleep in somebody's doorway, in icy rain and snow. I see myself, with my various physical challenges, unable to get the medications I need or the right kind of food. As for the cold, I'm already cold all the time except in summer.

I truly cannot comprehend what life is like for those with no home, but I do know it's terrible. I believe we, as a society, need to do more.

We are, after all, a nation, state, city, where a huge majority of us claim to believe in God and call ourselves Christians.

Where is our compassion?

~The Political Is Spiritual~

When Christian preachers say, "Jesus died for our sins," our lack of compassion is our greatest sin.

Jesus was compassion in action. His whole life models compassion, and He tells us that the ultimate standard with which He judges us is compassion. To those who act compassionately He says that when He was hungry, thirsty, a stranger, naked, sick or in prison, they gave Him what He needed, food, water, a place to stay, clothing, care and visits.

But the compassionate don't remember doing these things for Jesus. So Jesus answers them, "Truly I tell you, just as you did it to one of the least of these, you did it to me." Matthew 25:31-45.

But Jesus sends those who are not compassionate, those who see others' needs and are unwilling to help, into the eternal outer darkness.

I don't claim that solving homelessness is easy. I do believe that it will take community commitment to examine the harsh social, economic and spiritual costs of homelessness, not just their effect on the homeless but their impact on all of us.

I pray that our communities will come together and act, even as we continue to do our individual acts of compassion. In both ways we reveal our faith, in caring for the least of these.

~At the Water's Edge~

'

TELL ME THE STORIES

6

The Stuff of Life

I'm a lover of stories. As a child I wrote my first story about an Indian princess whose sweetheart went away and who knelt beside a lake and wept tears that became water lily pads. I've always believed that I made that story up, though sometimes I wonder if I read it someplace. I only know I had a startlingly vivid image in my head of the sorrowing princess, the lake and the lovely lily pads she created.

Stories, I'm convinced, are the stuff of life. Long before we had radio, TV, movies, video, computers, Ipods, and all the other media and devices that can bring us stories, people sat around campfires and told stories. These were stories about how the world began, about the mysterious powers that seemed to govern how things were, where people came from — all the great themes that continue to occupy scientists, artists and theologians even today.

No one knows how those ancient stories started, but they were passed along as true. I'm reminded of the native storytellers who begin their tales with, "This story is true, though it never happened." Truth resides in the meanings of the stories, not their factuality.

These stories imparted generations of wisdom to those who came after. The stories told people how to live, how to love, how to honor God and each other, and what was good and not good.

Some of the stories found their way into the Bible. The origins of stories like Jacob and Daniel are lost in the mists of time and I don't know how factual they are. I do know they're true.

The Jesus stories came later and multiple sources attest to Jesus' life, death and resurrection. We don't have a lot of facts, but we do have some.

Even so, what matters most to me about the Jesus stories is their truth in my life and the lives of others, their richness in bringing new life to those on the verge of spiritual death, as I once was. That is the truth I cling to, the truth that lights my darkest hours, strengthens my faith and moves me toward God.

Faith, says Hebrews 11:1, "is the assurance of things hoped for, the conviction of things not seen." My growing faith is what reveals the truth in Jesus Christ that I have not seen before. The pattern I've discovered is that as my faith grows, so does my ability to see more truth in Jesus. The process is a spiral, not a circle. Growing spiritually allows me to grow more.

As I tell the stories of my own life, I am constantly looking for where my stories intersect with the stories of the Bible, particularly the Jesus stories. Those intersections are where I learn about myself and what God asks of me.

Telling the story of my own life is my grand adventure. I want my life to be infused and informed with the stories of the Bible. That's why I love to hear the old, old stories again and again.

"Tell me the stories of Jesus," we sing. My heart shouts, "Yes! Tell me the stories forever."

Not Safe, But Very Good

My favorite scene in C.S. Lewis' *The Lion, the Witch and the Wardrobe* isn't in the movie.

The scene happens when the Pevensie children stumble through an old wardrobe into the magical land of Narnia, a land trapped in winter for one hundred years by the evil White Witch.

The children meet Mr. and Mrs. Beaver, who believe that these human children have come to fulfill a prophecy heralding the fall of the White Witch.

The Beavers have heard rumors that Aslan is coming back, Aslan the great lion, Lewis' Christ figure, who will return to set Narnia free.

After being told that Aslan is a lion, the elder sister Susan says, "Ooh! Is he — quite safe?"

Mrs. Beaver says, "If there's anyone who can appear before Aslan without their knees knocking, they're either braver than most or else just silly."

Little Lucy says, "Then he isn't safe?"

Mr. Beaver says, "Safe? Who said anything about safe? But he's good."

Not safe but good.

It took me many years to realize that Jesus is not safe, that he supports the weak and oppressed, and gets tough with the greedy, even overturning money-changers' tables. It's this strong Jesus who says to his disciples, "If any want to become my followers, let them deny themselves and take up their cross and follow me." Matthew 16:24.

In Sunday school, though, the Jesus I met was uniformly good, gentle and kind, and almost always pictured with happy children or lambs. My Sunday school Jesus was, with all the good intentions of the adults, too sweet and maybe even saccharine.

For reasons I don't understand, I felt differently about

God. God was mysterious, unknowable, Spirit, yet he was also pictured like Michelangelo's God, as a muscular, vigorous old man with a flowing white beard. I believed that God could change His aspect at will, becoming Jesus, the Holy Spirit, a dove or anything. I didn't understand how this could be, but I accepted it because I learned it from people I trusted. I loved this mysterious God.

But I didn't see the dangerous, mysterious Jesus, who says, "Those who want to save their life will lose it, and those who lose their life for my sake will find it," Matthew 16:25, or the Jesus who turns his face to Jerusalem and goes to confront the powerful religious and imperial authorities of the day, knowing that he will not leave the city alive.

I abandoned the church of my childhood partly because Jesus seemed so safe that he was boring and irrelevant. This was during the Civil Rights Movement, what the movement leaders called the Freedom Movement. The movement arose in the American South soon after *Brown* v. *Board of Education* (1954), which held that separate schools for black and white students are inherently unequal. I was passionately pro integration and I couldn't spot Jesus anywhere on the scene. He was there, but I couldn't see him.

In fact, Jesus was leading those Freedom Movement marches, and eventually I came to understand that. That was when I met the Jesus I love. This Jesus is very good, but never quite safe.

Smartest Guy in the Room

About five years ago I was having a haircut when the beautician started explaining how, the past Sunday, her pastor preached on the dangers of thinking too much about religious issues. "It leads people astray," she said, "and makes room for the devil to sneak into your heart. The pastor knows the truth and has to teach us."

Then she asked the most terrifying question that I never wanted to hear from a woman poised with scissors in her hand: "Don't you agree?"

I was neither brave nor quick-witted that day. I stifled my true response: "God created us with fine brains so we could use them." Instead I mumbled something about coming from a different tradition. The next month I found a new beauty shop, where I, pastor of a busy, active church, could relax and talk about kids and dogs.

My disagreement was not superficial. Jesus says, "You shall love . . . God with all your heart . . . soul . . . and mind…" Matt. 22:37. My church teaches that it's our theological duty to think about our faith. Our tools are the Bible, church tradition, our own and others' experience, and our reason. These are, we believe, essential for opening ourselves to the grace that leads first to a rich spiritual life and ultimately to salvation.

I am intrigued by what I see as the awesome intelligence of Jesus Christ. I see his intelligence in what he taught, and in how he taught in parables, forcing people to think about what his parables meant. Nor did he teach the familiar truths of his time, but rather saw through the familiar to God's eternal compassion: "You have heard that it was said, 'An eye for an eye and a tooth for a tooth.' But I say to you, Do not resist an evildoer." Matthew 5:38-39. He understood how violence leads to more violence, and so, as Gandhi put it, we all end up blind and toothless.

When, after Jesus' arrest, Pilate asked, "Are you the king of the Jews?" Jesus answered only, "You say so." He refused to fall into Pilate's trap by either affirming or denying, thus also removing any easy decision by Pilate about what to do with him.

I'm aware that people vary widely in how we approach faith issues. Some value certainties, like my beautician, happy when her pastor told her what to think. Some of us, though, believe that a life of faith requires active mental participation, as both an opening and a response to grace.

Sometimes grace prompts me to ask the very questions that can plunge me into doubt. This forces me to think more deeply and fearlessly about possible answers, ultimately enabling my spiritual growth. This process requires me to test anything claiming to be eternal truth.

I believe God gave us brains so we can sort the Godly from what is false, easy, conventional or convenient. Jesus, grace-filled and always the smartest guy in the room, models with his life, death and resurrection the way we are to do this.

Story of the Christmas Nail

Dear friends once gave us a special Christmas tree ornament, which hangs on our tree each year. It is our Christmas nail. It's steel, eight inches long, with a point at one end and a ribbon at the other.

A nail. Of all our ornaments, it means the most to me. The story goes like this. Once upon a time a baby was born to Jewish parents in Bethlehem. Maybe there were angels singing and shepherds watching their flocks by night, as told by Luke. And maybe there were wise men from the east bearing gifts for this child, as described by Matthew.

The child grew into a remarkable man who spent from one to three years in ministry, walking around the country-side gathering disciples, teaching, healing, and driving out demons. At this time Judea was a Roman-occupied province and the Jewish leaders were appointees of Rome.

These leaders became very worried when they heard about this teacher and his miracles. They thought, because there was much political foment in Judea in those days, that he probably meant to lead a rebellion against Rome. It wouldn't be the first rebellion they'd had to put down.

Near the end of his ministry, this remarkable, miracle-working man turned his steps to Jerusalem, the capitol of Judea, and walked right into the temple where he confronted the leaders and called them liars and hypocrites. The leaders reacted as powerful people often do when confronted with wrongs they've done. They moved to protect their power by getting rid of the person speaking out.

They arrested him, tried him and crucified him on a cross made from a tree, where, as Luke tells us, he said before he died, "Father, forgive them, for they don't know what they're doing." He died and was raised from the dead, the resurrected Christ, the Prince of Peace, for whom Christmas is named.

In the Christmas tree and the joy of that child's birth, Christians recall the nails driven into the hands and feet of the man Jesus as he was fastened to the cross. He could have run from persecution, or retaliated in kind, but instead he obeyed God's will in speaking truth to power even to the point of death.

Our lowly nail means all of that to me, and more. It

hangs close to the trunk of our tree because the outer limbs are too flimsy to support it. It is a dark, heavy nail and yet beautiful, because it speaks of forgiveness and redemption. "Father, forgive them for they don't know what they're doing." Even to the point of death and beyond. Forgive them. Break the cycle of hatred and violence by refusing to take part. Forgive those who persecute you, and turn the other cheek when struck. Stand for peace and God's justice in the face of crushing human injustice and armed conflicts. For me that is the Christmas nail, which shines eternally with the light of Christ's love, bringing new life for all.

What God Is This?

How I understand God makes a huge difference in my life. If God is all about fear, I think in terms of how evil needs to be punished. But if God is love, I am challenged by God always to grow in compassion.

I met Hal and Grace, a gracious and loving couple, in my husband's first church in another state. Some years earlier, their only child, not yet forty, had died of cancer. They were devastated. To make matters worse, certain people in their church at that time, instead of grieving with them and consoling them, said things like, "Too bad about Joy; if her faith had been strong enough, she would have lived." "Joy obviously was a sinner whose sins were well hidden."

During the time I knew Hal and Grace, they were stalwarts of their tiny church. No matter how people had treated them or their daughter, they had forgiven and moved on. In their late 70s, they rarely missed a Sunday in worship, always gentle and upbeat as my husband, in his final year in seminary, learned from them and others how to be a pastor. Grace was a soft-spoken spiritual powerhouse and chair of the church's governing body, active in the many church activities. She loved to say, "We're small but mighty."

Then Hal, a retired railroad man, had a stroke and was confined to a wheelchair. He could no longer climb the stairs to the worship space. First my husband and the other men tried to carry him up — and almost dropped him. After that, Hal sat patiently and listened to the service in the basement fellowship hall, until he became too ill to attend. Grace kept coming, though, serving as an inspiration to all of us.

Hal and Grace's God is a loving God, the God of "turn the other cheek," who sent Jesus not to call saints but sinners, who has special concern for those who exist on the margins of their societies and commands that they be cared for. This is the God of 1 John 4:7-8: "Beloved, let us love one another, because love is from God; everyone who loves is born of God and knows God. Whoever does not love does not know God, for God is love."

So who do I worship? A God of fear, who watches me like a hawk, waiting to pounce with hideous punishments for my great and minor missteps, my hidden sins? Or the God of infinite love, patience and mercy, the God of the Jesus who said from the cross, "Father, forgive them for they don't know what they are doing"?

This God is love, the unending love beyond human comprehension, the love that is not a feeling but is simply compassion in action.

Grace and Hal knew God well, and modeled what they knew in their lives. They taught my husband and me well. I am grateful, and theirs is the God I worship.

Grace at Work

Children's lives and well-being are so precious, and rearing them is a challenge. Recently my elder grandson, age seventeen, spent a month backpacking in the Alaskan wilderness with other young people his age, through the National Outdoor Leadership School (NOLS).

My daughter agonized about letting him go. They live in Virginia, a long way from Alaska. His not-brightest idea was, since he had his driver's license and a car, that his parents should allow him to drive from Virginia to Alaska by himself and back home again. His parents squashed that one right away. They take their job of getting him raised up in one piece very seriously.

I remember the fall day when my elder son was not yet two and my older daughter, now the mother of this Alaska-trekking boy, was three. I put both children down for naps, and then I, the perpetually tired mommy, lay down too. Oh, bliss. I dozed right off.

I woke up that afternoon sensing that something was horribly wrong. I ran to check the children. My daughter was there, asleep and looking damp and sweet.

My son was not in his bed, not anywhere in the house. I checked closets and under beds. My heart thumped wildly in my mouth.

I ran through the house and finally noticed the front door ajar. I raced outside, across the front porch and down the steps to the sidewalk.

This was an older, Midwestern neighborhood where the streets were laid out on a grid. The street in front of us was not very busy, few cars day or night.

But the street at the end of the block, one house away, was a thoroughfare, only two lanes but with a constant stream of traffic.

To my horror as traffic parted, I saw my boy, my darling little boy, on the other side of the street, standing there in his sleeper, his golden hair all tousled.

As I watched, he took a step toward me and my heart nearly stopped. If he came toward me, he walked right into traffic. Would anybody see him?

"Stay there, honey," I screamed, "Mommy's coming. Stay there, stay there…"

I ran faster than I knew I could, motioning for him to wait. A miracle — he listened to me and didn't move.

I don't know if drivers saw us and stopped, or if the traffic just parted like the Red Sea. I just know I never broke my stride getting across that street and scooping my boy into my arms.

I was crying so hard I couldn't see. It seemed like ten minutes before there was a break in the traffic and we could cross the street and go home.

I would never have thought that child could operate our front door lock. It just never occurred to me. And I almost lost my precious son.

Someone once said God made mothers because God cannot be everywhere at once.

I'd amend that a little bit. I'd say God made parents and other grown-ups because, even though God is everywhere all the time, God cannot act without the help of human hands.

A recent newspaper article told of a sharp-eyed woman

who spotted smoke coming from a car and noticed two small children left in that car. She and the two men she alerted, who acted so quickly to break into the car and pull the children out, and everyone else who offered assistance, are heroes in my book. They were God's eyes and hands in action. God bless and keep every one of them.

Bad Slip Day

Once I worked in the governor's office as a lawyer. I was feeling my oats and so I bought myself a beautiful, expensive woolen suit. It was the loveliest outfit I'd had in years.

I felt so good when I wore it, ready for anything. I could leap tall buildings at a single bound. I was young and couldn't believe that life has any limits.

That particular autumn day I wore my wonderful suit to work. I worked late, until everyone else had gone. Those were pre-security days and I didn't see a soul when I exited the Capitol's back door and cut across the lawn toward my car. Outside was still bright daylight.

I was halfway across this large expanse of grass when I felt something peculiar at my waist. I stopped, trying to figure it out. That was when the elastic of the old half-slip I was wearing gave up its grip. My slip dropped to the grass around my feet.

For an instant I was paralyzed with embarrassment. I stood still, shifting my eyes to look around, wondering if someone was watching me. I didn't see anyone.

Gulp. What to do?

In one hopefully fluid movement I stepped out of the poor washed-to-death slip, bent down and crammed it into my briefcase. I continued walking, head high, shoulders back, as if nothing had happened.

My cheeks flamed, though, and when I got to my car I sat inside for a few minutes, looking around for anyone watching.

Eventually I drove away, my embarrassment trailing behind, feeling as conspicuous as if tin cans had been tied to my bumper.

Why was I so discomfited? Did I think somehow that the incident revealed the real me? That under the spiffy suit and shiny high heels I was actually an unworthy person in tattered underwear?

Probably. During my early adolescence I was a pretty good kid, but I sometimes sassed my mother, ignored my chores and hung out around our suburban neighborhood with other kids instead of studying.

What I remember most about my dad's discipline during those years is a comment he often made when he came upon my many flaws. "Well, now we see the real Joan."

I know my dad loved me and didn't expect those remarks to affect me so profoundly, but they did. Eventually I started seeing myself as a "bad person" who needed to hide under plenty of nice-looking camouflage.

When my slip fluttered to the Capitol lawn that day, I became that young girl again. The unseen watcher I scanned for was my father.

Later I came to know an unfailingly gracious Father, a God who can always be counted upon to love me exactly as I am, raggedy underwear and all.

That Father embraced me as a beloved and taught me to understand and forgive both my dad's careless words and my anger that lasted for years. Now I suspect that Dad only did what was once done to him.

And I'm not even touchy about half-slips.

My Favorite Bible Scholar

MarySue joined my husband's first church in Boulder, Colorado. She called herself a conservative evangelical Christian, and she said she was searching for something.

She had heard lots of preaching that claimed to be biblical. She was so knowledgeable about the whole Bible, though, that some preachers upset her by making too many assertions that she couldn't find anywhere in her Bible.

Thus she arrived at our church.

We welcomed her warmly. She was great in meetings and classes. She always had a clear, well-articulated point of view that was enough different from mine that she challenged me to think and grow.

I was a seminary student then and I wanted to drag her to school with me. She had so much to offer. We never made it, which was my and the other students' loss.

MarySue was one of the most biblically literate people I've ever known. She'd memorized a good bit of the Bible, and you couldn't mention a story or verse that she didn't know.

Her Bible was marked with all kinds of colors and underlinings, tabs and notes. I remember someone telling me once that it was sinful to write in a Bible. Evidently that person never got hold of MarySue.

"Every year," she said, "I pick a theme and I read all the way through the Bible studying that theme. You can't imagine all that I've discovered."

Simply astonishing. No one could fool her with inch-deep biblical knowledge even if it looked a mile wide.

MarySue grew up poor and had to work very hard to raise her family. Yet she never neglected her beloved Bible.

One time not long after she joined us, she told me of a

remarkable dream she'd had.

"I was in this huge green field," she said, "and there was a fence around me, fairly close to me. As I watched, the fence started slowly moving outward, way out toward the horizon where I could hardly see it."

"What do you think it means?" I asked.

"I don't know," she said. "Maybe it means my horizons are expanding."

That year her annual study was on the nature of God.

"Did you know," she asked excitedly one day, "that God changes? So far I've read from Genesis to Luke, and there are lots of changes. Some are because of Jesus, but I also think people became better able to understand God's nature."

She often came up with such things and they were stunning. She had no truck with finding someone to tell her what the Bible says. She figured that the Bible is God's word, so she should experience God's word for herself.

She waded in fearlessly and patiently to explore the Bible's great themes, without struggling to maintain her preconceived ideas. She let the Holy Spirit guide her reading, and the Holy Spirit opened fabulous vistas of faith and truth before her.

I owe much of my love of the Bible to MarySue. She was, for me, God's genuine gift.

~At the Water's Edge~

COMMUNITY MATTERS

7

Loving the Imperfect Community

During worship one Sunday, I watched a pastor friend baptize a nine-year-old boy. I was taken with what she said to him. "I am so happy to baptize you today," she said. "But I have to tell you, the church is not perfect and a time may come when it lets you down. That can happen even when it's trying not to, because it's made of imperfect people like me. The thing to do then is to hang on, and, if you possibly can, forgive." Then she added, "God loves you, I love you, and the church loves you. Only God's love is perfect."

This boy was being reared by a single mom who worked a minimum wage job. Every few months a new man was in the house, and the only real stability the boy knew was with his grandmother, the one who brought him to church.

The church is made up of human beings, and I agreed completely with my pastor friend. Churches let people down all the time in many ways, even when all the people involved have the very best intentions. The boy had come to love this pastor, and she knew that most of the people in his life had already let him down many times. She hoped that by telling the boy the truth of churches, he would stay engaged when something happened that angered him, as it almost certainly would.

At the beginning of my teen years, I remember thinking that the church I grew up in no longer had a place for me. I'd been attached to that church since early childhood, and my heart still has a warm place for it. But when I was thirteen, I perceived that it would only accept me if I changed to be how I was "supposed" to be, obedient, unquestioning and well-disciplined. I could be all of those things, but none of them very consistently.

I no longer felt welcomed and I started looking for the door. I found it four years later when I moved into a college dorm in another town. For twenty years I showed up in church only on an occasional Christmas.

Churches are no different now, I perceive. All those I've known personally are very warm, open and loving in some ways and can be closed and hard in others. Their ways of being open and closed differ widely from denomination to denomination and even from church to church within the same communion.

Yet church remains my model for true community, a place where people can care for each other and treat each other with love and dignity. Church community was where I first sat around a table and looked at all the faces, knowing that I'd come to love them, these people who were barely acquaintances a few weeks earlier. Christ Jesus turns us into a new kind of friend through him.

Community, I believe, is what makes us fully human. It's the place outside our families where we learn give and take, and, if it's a good community, how to be loving and respectful to others and to ourselves.

God may be found in the isolation and grandeur of mountains, or in the beauty of a sunrise. But for Jesus you need community, which means other people.

Jesus goes where the people are, especially the poor, the suffering, the aged, the lame, the children, the powerless. Jesus wants us to find him and love him in the faces of everyone we meet.

Community is the only place we can learn to do that, because it never happens in the abstract. We can read about it in books, or think, talk or write about it all by ourselves. But to really do it and be it, we have to meet face to face.

My pastor friend is a remarkably loving, insightful and generous person. I once heard a woman say, after accompanying her on home visits to shut-ins, "It's like sitting at the feet of Jesus."

This pastor brought a powerful sense of community to everything she did. She is one of those who taught me that community is our life together. When it is grounded in Jesus it is better than just about anything else.

Tiny Bubbles

Recently I've been reading *Talk to the Hand*, by Lynne Truss, subtitled *The Utter Bloody Rudeness of the World Today, or Six Good Reasons to Stay Home and Bolt the Door*. I first heard the enchanting phrase "talk to the hand" from an unlikely source, our then four-year-old granddaughter. It was accompanied by a palm flung up toward our faces as she walked away from us. Evidently she wasn't into the conversation we thought we were having.

"Talk to the hand" is hilarious in a four-year-old, especially if you've never heard it before, but I think it's best to hide the laugh. Four-year-olds have a way of growing up, and what's side-splitting in a little one can morph into teeth-grinding annoyance in adolescents or adults.

Truss laments many kinds of rudeness, but her bottom

line is that "rudeness is a moral issue and always has been. The way people behave toward each other, even in minor things, is a measure of their value as human beings." It's really about public morality, or "the common good," not a phrase we hear much nowadays. "Bad manners," Truss writes, "lead to other kinds of badness. If we each let the 'FOR THE COMMON GOOD' bit of our brains shrivel on the vine, the ultimate result is crime, alienation and moral hell."

Picture a large intersection in Denver, five lanes from each direction. We were waiting in a left-turn lane when a young woman whizzed past us into the center of the intersection, only to find two walls of metal charging at her from left and right. Without missing a beat, she slammed into reverse and backed up at high speed coming to rest beside us.

My heart was in my mouth. I'm glad nobody had pulled up behind her and that she didn't swerve a little to the left or right. The young woman seemed unaffected. No harm done, after all. The terrible things that could have happened didn't. She was bouncing inside her car to her own beat, inside her own little solipsistic bubble. I had the impression that all the rest of us at that busy intersection barely existed for her.

It isn't such a long way from that young woman's

behavior to kids smashing windshields and mail boxes. And from there it isn't very far to the shooting we saw on York Road last year, here in Helena, Montana, when a couple of young people pumped bullets into a car carrying a mother and child.

Why would anyone do that? Most of us find it incomprehensible. But I think a breakdown happens when we start living in solipsistic bubbles, our "personal space" where I'm my only reality and only my wants and needs count.

I realize that the problem goes deeper than good manners, but we really do need to get rid of those tiny bubbles of self-importance. As Truss points out, it's about how we value each other. Our behavior shows kindness or contempt. As we go, so goes our community and our world. Guess I better climb out of my bubble right now, and maybe paint "FOR THE COMMON GOOD" on my forehead.

Ending Homelessness

It's clear to me that caring for the poor is a religious duty. This is what speaks loudest to me from the Sermon on the Mount (Matt. Ch. 5-7), believed by many to be the greatest religious writing ever.

That's why, when I was a pastor in Littleton,

Colorado, I took my youth group for a "homeless tour" in downtown Denver. First we walked several blocks to a shelter providing free beds for a few nights, where everyone had to be out by 8 a.m. Then we trekked a mile to the breakfast site, and on to a small grassy space where many homeless people spent their days. Dinner was another mile away.

Our tour guide was Arvin, a homeless man whose skin was weathered from living mostly outside, and who, in late May, wore all his tattered clothing, including his coat, because he had no place else to keep things.

Arvin was white, about forty, medium height with light-colored hair. He said he'd lost his home and a good job because of alcoholism, but now he'd been sober for several years, was working for the Denver agency that arranged our tour, and had saved almost enough money to rent an apartment. We bought him lunch and gave him $25 for his time.

I recalled Arvin when I read a recent newspaper editorial on homelessness. It brought tears of hope to my eyes. The editorial mentioned Philip Mangano, head of the U.S. Interagency Council on Homelessless, who is traveling the country to help start programs to end chronic homelessness. He spoke in Billings to a group planning to end homelessness there within ten years.

Mangano cites U.S. studies that consistently show the cost for homeless services at about a third higher than it would be if the homeless were given their own apartments.

One Boston study showed that 119 chronically home-less people made 18,000 hospital emergency room visits during the study period averaging $1,000 per visit. So I ran some numbers. 18,000 at $1,000 each is $18,000,000. If 119 people are housed at $700 a month, the annual cost is $999,600, just under a million, leaving many millions for other services and still costing less than the homeless emer-gency room visits.

Mangano provides a fine example of how compassion, common sense and good economics can coincide. But we've been passing through an era when compassion has seemed downright foolish, where the nineteenth century concern only for the "deserving poor," those who were clearly with-out fault in their own poverty, has morphed into a concern that if we give people what they desperately need, they will immediately turn greedy, lazy and shiftless. Maybe a few do. But I believe the facts show that most able-bodied, mental-ly competent adults, if given a leg up, will work hard to stand on their own.

You see, I can't forget that when Jesus sorts the sheep from the goats, the deciding factor isn't "just deserts." It's how we treated "the least of these."

Time In

I once heard a pastor thank his congregation for taking time out for church. I realized that for me church isn't so much "time out" as "time in."

It's "time in" a place that to me is holy, where I often encounter God. That's when time for me suspends — I stop hearing it click past as I usually do. At those moments I find myself floating in what feels like eternity, where love governs all and death is an illusion. Though it doesn't happen often, it's worth all my involvement and participation.

Church for me is also "time in" a quiet place where silence and contemplation are usually encouraged. Most worship services I've attended provide for silent prayer or moments of meditation, hopefully for more than ten seconds. In our age of constant stimulation and split-second imagery, I yearn to tune out the world and listen for what is deeper than sighs.

Church is "time in" for me, too, because I'm with like-minded people. I don't mean that people of specific churches all think alike. Far from it. I've heard in many churches, "Put ten of us together and you get ten different opinions about almost everything." But most will listen to each other, care about similar things, and are willing to think and dream and even work toward them.

I can't say I find all of this "time in" each time I come to church. I wish I did. But sometimes I come with negative emotions in my heart. The worship service usually dissipates those feelings very quickly — but not always. That means I'm not emotionally available to receive what I came for. Some days I'm just out of sorts.

But I do believe that much of what I find in church is intimately tied to what I bring with me. If I'm open, loving, responsive, my "time in" sings. If not, well, that day I usually kind of miss out.

Having said that, though, I also believe that the things I seek in church are pretty much always there waiting for me and others. They don't go away just because I'm distracted, unresponsive, or emotionally closed.

I need my "time in" a church's holy spaces. On the best days, it puts me in touch with the things that really matter, the abundant life that Jesus speaks of in John 10:10. It makes my heart feel loving, welcoming and forgiving. Sometimes it's hard — though necessary — to return to what we usually call "the real world."

My "time in" reminds me that God is ultimately in charge. Sometimes, watching world events and even events closer to home, it's difficult to remember that. My "time in" washes away my fear and cynicism and gives me hope.

So for me it's "time in" with God, not "time out." I

can have it anywhere, but church is special. It is holy time, it restores my soul and inspires me to carry my "time in" out to the world again.

Get Rich Quick?

An obnoxious email arrived this week. If I would partner up with "Mrs. Nancy Brooks" of "National Westminster Bank UK" and follow her instructions, I could receive 35 percent of $12,600,000. That's $4,410,000.

The big number, twelve million, was no doubt in the first line of the email to crank up my greed. Then followed the sad, sad story of why the sender has access to the money.

It seems a poor Kruger Gold Co. miner in South Africa, who also happened to be a geologist, deposited the money in "Mrs. Brooks's" bank. This poor fellow was soon killed in a "ghastly motor accident," leaving no next-of-kin or after-death instructions.

If I would only be reliable and trustworthy and do what they asked . . . .

This email bothered me. First I called Consumer Protection at the Attorney General's office for their email address and forwarded this one. Next, doing my own little investigation, I went online.

I learned that the National Westminster Bank UK is a

web site which offers to lend money. I couldn't find any physical location or quick way to test its authenticity.

I discovered many people named Nancy Brooks, including a professor, a litigator, an artist, and an air national guard colonel. Obviously none of them are this "Nancy Brooks."

Finally I googled Kruger Gold Company and obtained lots of information about this scam. It's obviously been around for a while, and the phony miner is variously named Andrea Smith, Mr. Smith B. Andreas, and Fernando Carlos.

I'm usually not very suspicious. Thus I've sometimes been taken. But I'm not very greedy either, so the ones that get me are usually spurious schemes to help someone.

I don't often get angry about those things, even if they're sometimes embarrassing and costly. I truly believe Jesus' teaching about how I'm supposed to love my neighbor as myself, and Jesus never applied that teaching only to the "deserving." As a matter of fact, he taught the opposite. Everybody loves their family and friends, he said, "But I say to you, Love your enemies and pray for those who persecute you...." Matt. 5:44. I seem also to recall something about forgiving those who trespass against me.

That doesn't mean I can ignore scam artists. This is the first email like this I've ever received. Oh, I used to get the investment ads, the girls-girls-girls and others more disgusting. I hoped to see the end of it. But I believe in free access to the internet, and that means all kinds can get in.

I did what I could with this email, though it still distresses me because it was obviously intended to rip off the unsuspecting. It was so transparent, yet I couldn't believe the scammers would keep using it if it didn't occasionally work.

So I said some prayers for all intended victims. Then, knowing God works in ways I can't imagine, I said more prayers for the scammers to undergo big changes of heart.

Speeding Ticket

I got my first and only speeding ticket four years ago, in a little western Colorado town. I was visiting my church leaders to tell them I was ill and had to retire.

My first visit was to Dell who lives up a long, winding road in the Colorado mountains. He, his wife and I were good friends and I stayed too long. Suddenly I realized that it was time for my next appointment.

As I hurried to my car, a propane truck pulled in and started filling their tank, blocking the only exit. I had no choice, so I waited. Then I was late. I sped toward home to meet Sandy, my next appointment.

I heard the siren, pulled over and a pleasant young officer came to my window. I burbled how sorry I was and started telling him about my tough day.

"Stop," he said, holding up his hand, "you're almost making me feel sorry." I think he was new and being trained, because I saw our chief in the police car silently laughing his face off.

Embarrassed, I took my ticket, and drove demurely the two blocks home, where Sandy was already gone.

I'm still a little embarrassed about that ticket, and the big question is why.

When he heard about my speeding ticket Dell, a retired big city police officer, laughed. He told me about driving from Colorado to the west coast in a day, and not starting all that early.

I asked, "Don't you ever get stopped?" He just flashed me that big grin of his. Hmmm.

Sandy laughed too. When they noticed my embarrassment, they laughed harder. Sandy said, "You wouldn't believe how many speeding tickets I've had."

Why should I care so much about that ticket when wonderful people like Dell and Sandy blow them off?

Is there still a little girl in me that thinks people won't love me if I do something wrong? Probably, but she's hiding behind a lot of theological shrubbery.

The real reason, I suspect, is that I see all parts of life

as relating to all other parts of life. It's like the huge celestial net I once saw in a kind of vision, connecting everything and everyone in the universe.

That web connects me to God, and I value that connection more than anything else in life. I can't bear to disrupt it.

I thought I had good reasons to speed that day. I was late, Sandy was waiting, I love her and didn't want to be rude to her.

All well and good.

But I was also upset, not very well and rushing too fast. I lost my ability to recognize that Sandy would have no trouble forgiving me for being late.

I was not being my best self, the person God created me to be. I know that I, like all of us, am God's beloved even when I mess up. I let my frazzle disrupt my connection with God and speeding was the result.

There. Maybe now I can forget about it.

Trick-or-Treat

Halloween has come and gone and I didn't trick-or-treat this year. My costume was "recovering surgical patient," complete with walker and shiny new hip. I'm recovering well and working hard to get back on my feet.

~At the Water's Edge~

I got out of the hospital the weekend before Halloween and had to miss the Halloween party with some of my grandchildren, but I cherish the invitation. I couldn't walk to the door to hand out candy to our neighborhood kids either, but my husband did. And I enjoyed hugging the grandchild who came bouncing in to show me her wonderful clown costume.

There is one more special way that I participated in Halloween this year. For weeks I collected quantities of loose change, not to add to the Halloween economy but for one of my favorite fundraisers.

You've probably seen those cute little orange boxes that appear every fall: Trick-or-Treat for UNICEF, the United Nations' Children's Fund.

This year I watched the Trick-or-Treat for UNICEF DVD twice. It's marvelous and I wish everyone could see it. This is kids helping kids, something that most young people are very good at.

Most children's hearts are soft, with a softness straight from God. Their eyes are clear, with the clarity that can see suffering in others, care deeply and respond accordingly.

This is why I think Jesus said, "Let the little children come to me, and do not stop them; for it is to such as these that the kingdom of heaven belongs." Matthew 19:14. Children with soft hearts and clear eyes make a real difference in the world. So do adults with those same character-istics.

Trick-or-Treat for UNICEF began in 1950. Now many of those first generation UNICEF Trick-or-Treaters are grandparents. I hope their grandchildren are carrying on and enlarging this wonderful tradition.

So what does UNICEF fund with its little orange boxes? The boxes have four words on the front: water, health, nutrition, education.

Did you know that 10 million children die each year for the lack of basic necessities?

Recently UNICEF has helped children in the aftermath of the Pakistani earthquakes and in the midst of violence and starvation in the Congo and Darfur. It has assisted displaced families in Gaza, immunized many children in Afghanistan, and worked to educate children in Haiti. This only touches the surface of what UNICEF does.

UNICEF can treat pneumonia for 33 cents, immunize a child for $17, provide a year's worth of school supplies for 50 kids for $35, build a village well for $150.

So little does so much.

This year, in an unprecedented move, half of the money collected stays in the US to help children here, especially young Katrina victims.

I realize that not everyone supports the United

Nations, and I don't doubt that the UN has problems, as does every large, long-standing institution.

But UNICEF is for kids and it does a wonderful job. Kids helping kids. As it does every year, it touched my heart and my wallet.

Everlasting Arms

Recently I heard an interview with the father of a child who died in the 1999 Columbine shootings. He seems still in a rage, angry at the teenaged shooters, police and school. The Columbine father's years of outraged grieving seem extreme, but it isn't unusual for a victim's family members to suffer with pain and grief for the rest of their lives.

Since Columbine we've seen other school shootings. The most recent ones in Bailey, Colorado, and Nickel Mines, Pennsylvania, seem particularly horrible because they happened in lovely rural areas, committed by adult males against young girls.

Families and whole communities have been traumatized in the wake of these shootings. The great question for me is this: Is forgiveness and healing possible when the innocent are ravaged and destroyed?

I am profoundly moved by what is happening in Nickel Mines. The deeply religious Amish are responding with forgiveness and care for each other and also for the grieving shooter's family.

No vengeance here, no blaming God or outsiders, only tears, shared sorrow, compassion and reaching out.

You might think this little community was prepared for this. With their quiet ways of cooperation and kindness, horse-drawn buggies and candlelight, their lives proceed at the pace of a person or horse walking. They seek prayer and contentment, not speed or excitement.

This is not to say that their lives are easy. They work hard, often at tasks that I, with my modern appliances, can do at the touch of a button. There is no "easy button" in Amish communities.

And the life isn't for everyone. At the age of sixteen, Amish children are allowed to break loose, experiment with the temptations of the outside world. Then they have to make a clear choice, stay or go. Most but not all choose to stay.

The Amish did not withdraw from the world to protect themselves from violence. They aren't like the gated communities across America supposedly secure behind high walls and security guards.

The Amish withdrew to live in the footsteps of Jesus, supporting themselves by their own labor.

They would probably be the first to admit that they are

not perfect. Sometimes discontent boils up in Amish communities, and they too know the face of sin.

But they keep God and the teachings of Jesus Christ at their center, every day and in every possible way.

One reporter watched a mother prepare her own young daughter's body for burial. The mother is heartbroken, but she knows her baby is in God's care, and she too forgives.

That is possible because in her community forgiveness is the norm. Forgiveness is expected of a Jesus follower.

So the Amish mourners, who have no telephones or email, go from home to home on foot or in their buggies. They view the little girls laid out for burial, they weep and they forgive.

It is a magnificent lesson for the rest of us. What would our world be like if we were to learn to do likewise?

RESTORED
TO NEW LIFE

8

A Thin Veil

I look back at myself as a young woman and I have to laugh. I was so full of myself. I heard talk in church about new life, and I viewed it as somewhere between quaint and foolish. God, church, Christian renewal and life eternal belonged to my parents' and grandparents' generations.

It was the sixties after all, and hadn't my parents heard that God was dead? The "God is dead" idea came from the German philosopher Nietzsche, and I had friends who talked about Nietzsche endlessly.

Not that I bought into it. By that stage of my life, I didn't want to think about religion. My generation, I figured, was beyond it and I'd find my life's meaning elsewhere.

So I turned to Albert Camus, Algerian-French author

and philosopher. My favorite was his "Myth of Sisyphus." Poor Sisyphus is a figure from Classical mythology who endlessly has to roll a boulder up a hill. Then the boulder rolls down and Sisyphus must push it up again. Camus's point is that we humans need to find meaning in pushing that boulder up the hill, no matter that it looks like pointless activity.

I thought Camus was right. A friend once said, "If you want to be happy, you have to learn to like doing what you have to do anyway." I agreed and adopted the idea. It was my policy and it more or less worked, but it was not a joyful way to live.

Then one day I heard God calling me. I had lost myself in mazes of doubt, denial, and a kind of absurd I-can-do-it-myself pride. God was busy finding me. I wanted to be found.

I had no idea that renewal, new life — and eternal life — lay in the direction toward God. I only wanted to go there and I did. I'm still on the way. What happened was like a light starting to glow in my soul. Very soon the things inside me that had seemed dead or dying began to show new life.

Now I think the whole "God is dead" thing lies somewhere between quaint and presumptuous. God is the ultimate kindness, the regenerative force in our lives and the universe. I don't think God judges us or seeks retribution because we endlessly declare God this or that, though I wonder sometimes if God doesn't shed a tear or get a chuckle out of our astonishing hubris, as we presume to whittle God down to human size.

God is. The Unknowable, the Ineffable, the Alpha and the Omega, the One who was there at the beginning of everything, the One who will be there forever, the One who always makes all things new, including human beings.

God renews me constantly with the love of family and friends, the beauty of the earth, and the powerful connection I feel to God and Jesus Christ. Through surgery, when I was utterly helpless, God embraced me and lifted the veil for me briefly so that I could look ahead at what comes next and would not be afraid.

That veil, I learned, is very thin. Sometimes maybe it's even porous, and God, the always welcoming, eternal, living God, is on both sides.

I look back on myself in the sixties, and what I see is that my questioning and questing has brought me a long ways. It has never quite let me rest, saying, "Now I have the answers." God renews me, keeps calling and nudging me onward. There are vistas ahead that I have never dreamed. My faith is strong and my life is full of love and joy. God's blessings are without end.

Kite Mystery

The other afternoon my best friend's granddaughter brought her parents to fly kites with us. Our house is in a windy area and the wind was up. We had a roundish kite with a tail and they brought a butterfly kite.

I watched the kites soar and they took my heart with them. I remember as a child having dreams of flying that sometimes spilled over into my waking hours. I could actually see myself outside my body, whirling and soaring and diving like the birds.

One of my favorite places to do this was in church, where sitting still was always a challenge. I never told my parents my childish way of fighting boredom from sermons that I couldn't begin to understand.

As our kites tugged higher and higher, I drifted back almost three decades to the day some women friends and I went out to fly kites on what was then a big open field near the hospital.

That day was overcast, with clouds shuttling back and forth, and I recall that our kites flew so high we thought we might lose them. They became little dots in the distance. I was with people I loved, having a great time, and yet melancholy overcame me, and I couldn't figure out why.

~Restored to New Life~

The next day, as my family and I were getting ready to fly a kite Lowell had made, the phone rang. It was my father calling from Iowa. "Mommy's dead," he cried into the phone.

In that instant, the moment before I fully registered what Dad was saying, something flashed through my mind as vivid as a comet. Mom is not alone, Grandma is with her and she's just fine.

This thought embraced me with a deep and profound peace beyond anything I'd ever imagined. Only then did my grief hit. It hit so hard it nearly knocked me off my feet. Even so, that core of deep peace remained.

I had no idea where that comet came from. This was before my slow and halting return to the church, while I was still in my phase of rejecting God. Later, I came to understand.

Kites and my mother's death. For me the two are inextricably linked. I marvel that I still have moments of missing her so intensely after all these years, especially in springtime when I watch kites dancing in the wind.

This life, I've come to believe, is not all there is, and we grievously cheat ourselves if we live our lives thinking this life is the end. If we reject the promise of eternity, I believe we miss the full beauty and wonder of God's creation in this life. And, as we age, our souls may close up in fear rather than opening to the eternal radiance of God's love and glory.

> Someday I'll fly
> Like a kite in the sky,
> Whirling and dipping,
> And soaring so high.
> I'll taste the clouds
> And smell the day,
> The wind will blow harder
> And I'll fly away.

Prayer Shawl

After my heart surgery last year my friend Pat knitted me a beautiful prayer shawl with a prayer in every stitch. Pat was part of a prayer shawl ministry, and before she sent me the shawl, all the members wrapped themselves in my shawl and added their own prayers.

I treasure my prayer shawl. It's amply sized, and lovely in shades of purple and violet. It comforts me in moments when God seems so distant.

My shawl went through hard times during my early months of heart surgery recovery. I was nauseated for weeks and barfed more than once on my wonderful shawl. Half seriously I wondered if the prayers would wash out.

But no matter the washings, my shawl retains all its warmth, and the prayers continue to murmur just as they did when new.

As I improved, I no longer wore my prayer shawl day and night. I even grew a little impatient with it, and associated it with sitting still for days, healing while sunk in sleepiness and passivity. I washed my shawl, folded it neatly and put it away.

I remembered my shawl when I had to check into the hospital last October for a new hip. A mysterious Something led me to find it just waiting for me in its drawer. When I got home from the hospital, I was eager to put it on. I discovered that my shawl is still full of prayers and healing. The prayers have been whispering around my shoulders for the past weeks like a showering of grace.

Today is the first day I haven't worn my shawl. Soon I won't need it. I'll wash it and put it away, hopefully not to have to use it again for a long time.

Now I've started a prayer shawl for someone I love whom I want to bless with lots of prayers. She doesn't know about it yet, but I'm up to surprise her.

The shawl ministry book Pat sent me begins with this Bible verse: "You formed my inmost being; you knit me in my mother's womb." Psalm 139:13. In this book the wonderful knitting women who pass along the prayer shawl ministry are honoring the maternal side of God, the God who wants to watch over us like a hen watching over her chicks. Luke 13:34.

As I knit this prayer shawl for my friend, I too put a prayer in every stitch. The pattern is knit, knit, knit, purl, purl, purl, over and over. For each knit stitch I say, "God bless (my friend's name), and for each purl I say another short prayer such as, "God keep (name)." This is the pattern I repeat again and again.

As I continue knitting, though, my prayers change. They grow deeper, more creative and sometimes even mysterious. I'll be knitting along, praying, and find that I don't even understand the prayer I'm praying, except that it feels just right. And sometimes the knitting itself is so focused that it transports me and becomes its own kind of mystical, communion-with-God experience.

I may benefit from this shawl more than my friend does, because it fills my days with prayer and love for my friend. As I wear my shawl from Pat and knit my own for another friend, I feel grace all around me, comforting and healing.

No wonder I just interrupted my husband's work to say, "I feel so happy." And my heart said, "Amen."

Dragon Skins

In C.S. Lewis' *The Voyage of the Dawn Treader*, one of the main characters is a young prig named Eustace, a boy who is never happy. To his great dismay, one day Eustace gets sucked through a picture on his uncle's bedroom wall onto a Narnian sailing ship on a tossing sea.

Soon the ship is battered by a huge storm, and the crew must make repairs on a rather ominous-looking, unknown island. Lazy Eustace sneaks into the mountains to nap until the work is done, but gets lost in a great fog. He's terrified when a dragon creeps past him and dies.

Eustace spots the dragon's lair and enters, finding great treasures of gold, silver and jewels. He weighs himself down with riches that he wants to take away with him, but something makes him fall asleep.

Poor, silly Eustace. When he wakes up he discovers that he has become a dragon. He is uncomfortable in his thick, heavy skin and starts remembering how great it was to be a boy. He also begins realizing that he hasn't been as kind and pleasant to others as he might have been. Slowly, something akin to repentance begins to awaken in his heart.

Eventually the huge lion Aslan, Lewis' Christ figure, comes looking for the frightened and repenting Eustace. Aslan says, "Follow me," and Eustace follows the Great

Lion higher into the mountains. There, after a long time, they arrive at a lush garden, and in the middle is a large, bowl-shaped pool that rises from a deep well. Marble steps lead into the crystal clear water.

Aslan tells Eustace to get undressed and get in. Three times Eustace peels off his dragon skin only to find another layer of dragon skin underneath. He keeps peeling layers. Finally Aslan says, "You will have to let me undress you." In spite of his fear, Eustace lies down and yields to the lion's claws.

"The very first tear he made," Eustace says, "was so deep that I thought it had gone right into my heart. And when he began pulling the skin off, it hurt worse than anything I've ever felt."

But Aslan opens Eustace up and finally there Eustace is, a boy again, "as smooth and soft as a peeled switch." Aslan hurls Eustace into the water, which smarts for a moment and then becomes "perfectly delicious."

Eustace's pool, to me, is the pool of baptism, where newly baptized infants and adults become part of the body of Christ, and adults can find deep spiritual cleansing. Every enduring religion has ways of accomplishing these things. In Christianity Jesus is the one who will, if we permit, peel away for once and always our layers of dragon skin that otherwise will eventually imprison and choke our hearts.

I'm always mystified by people who say, "I'm very spiritual but want nothing to do with organized religion." I'm certainly aware of organized religion's mistakes and stupidities, not to mention its downright sins. Organized religion is full of garden-variety sinners like me. So I figure that's what you get.

But there's another side to this. I've found no other place where I can learn to trust so fully, to submit to a higher power, and to let the claws of the lion undress me, peeling off the old scaly skin and washing me in the water of new life.

Ashes to Joy

Sin? In this "I'm okay, you're okay" culture, who wants to talk about sin? I knew various definitions, such as "turning away from God," and the Bible's "thou shalts" and "shalt nots," all helpful. But I'd never looked fearlessly inside to see the truth about my own sinfulness.

Once my friend Frances was Sister Mary Francis, nun-in-training. She left her convent weeks before her final vows and later we met as seminary students.

Frances was well grounded in spiritual disciplines and the history, tradition and theology of the church. We had many theological discussions.

~At the Water's Edge~

She brought me up short one day when she said, "We can psychologize all we want, but it's really about sin."

Her remark shocked me and started me on the path to true spiritual growth. What I saw was how sin is like a virus that's invaded every cell of my body. I don't want it, most days I despise it, but even now I can turn self-righteous about things like poor restaurant service, or being snubbed or cut off in traffic.

Sin is hauntingly pervasive in my life. It isn't the obvious things. I don't commit murder or adultery, but I get snarky with my husband, another sin of self-righteousness. I don't carve wooden gods and worship them, but what are my idols? Perfectionism? A new computer or car? Maybe sometimes.

You get the drift. Much sin is subtle. It's exceedingly difficult to see in myself.

Coping with this "sin-virus" is a lifetime's work. It takes regular time spent in the great spiritual disciplines such as prayer, study, community worship, confession and repentance. As someone once said about prayer, "You have to show up." There are many ways to do the spiritual work. The point is to find ways that fit and do them.

So why would any busy person spend all this time and effort on spiritual growth? Because the benefits are phenomenal, though not always well known.

For starters, growing in spirit mitigates pain. It eases spiritual pain, the kind that drives people to drink, drugs, gangs, temper tantrums and other unhappy behaviors, maybe even war. It also can ease physical pain — I'm almost a poster-child for that, given my recent almost pain-free surgeries.

Spiritual growth opens up life and love and gives one the riches and joy of God's creation and deep human friendship. Its blessings are beyond compare.

These blessings are why I attend an Ash Wednesday service to begin Lent, the 40-day period, excluding Sundays, before Easter. The minister makes a cross of ashes on my forehead, saying, "Remember that you are dust, and to dust you shall return." I am grateful for this time of repentance, to acknowledge my mortality and meditate on eternal truths.

Life is so short. We want it to be rich and full. The path to abundant life passes through Ash Wednesday into Lent, and through Good Friday. It is the only way to God's joy, now and eternally. There's no way around, only through.

Sad, Sad Tail of Algaeman

For twenty years my husband Lowell and I have wanted a pond. A fish pond with koi and other fish in it.

~At the Water's Edge~

The time was never right. We were always living in a parsonage or on the brink of moving.

Finally in July Lowell grabbed a shovel and started digging. At last, at last. A pond.

The first thing he encountered was sand. Lots of it. When you dig through the thin crust of dirt in our yard, you get sand.

I once heard this area was part of Lake Missoula, the great prehistoric lake that covered much of this part of the country. If so, I'm betting we were the shallows or a beach.

Lowell built wooden frames so the sides of the pond wouldn't collapse, leveled everything, fitted in the underlayment and liner, filled it with water, and — voilà! A pond! A real pond!

We waited a few days, bought some little fish and put them in. Adorable creatures, graceful and bright. We ran outside at least three times a day to delight in watching them.

Ah, but little did we know, Algaeman was stalking our pond. We used a chemical to control the algae and went off for ten days of vacation.

When we returned our fish were healthy and active, but the water was greenish. Algae! While we were in Washington State, my sweetheart purchased a better algae control chemical.

Unfortunately he didn't read the labels, which said, "Kills fish." He dosed our pond and — oh, sadness — our fish died. Every last one. Algaeman had struck.

Lowell buried the fish, emptied the pond, cleaned it, refilled it — and we added more fish.

Little did we suspect what Algaeman was up to.

"Look," says Lowell, "I see more algae."

I should have said, "Keep your cotton-picking chemicals out of that pond." But I didn't.

This time he used the older chemical which hadn't hurt the fish, but he dumped in a double dose.

Yes, Algaeman struck again. All the fish died — again.

We groaned and cried and felt terrible. That lasted about a day. We waited a week, added new fish and they seem to be doing fine. Maybe Algaeman has departed.

I love our pond. I hope we get it right this time. All those years of ministry, I'd think of Jesus who, when the pressure of the crowds got too exhausting, withdrew to quiet places, preferably places with mountains and water. There he'd pray and restore his soul, re-energizing for the great works ahead of him.

Most days the troubles of the world are all too much with me. I hear names like Darfur, Iraq and New Orleans, I think of Jesus' love for all people and I want to weep.

I do what I can and it is so painfully little. Yet even I

need those times of prayer, meditation and restoration.

That is what our pond is to me. Mountains, water and the flashing tails of God's little fishes.

Algaeman, beware!

Easter Unspeakable

Sometimes generational differences are funny. Old Great Aunt Mary, aged ninety-five, is visibly failing. Yet we her juniors tiptoe around and pretend she'll get better because, gosh, maybe she hasn't noticed that she's 95 and dying. Are we scared to break the news? Do we assume she's afraid to die? Or do we just project our own fears on her?

I love it when Great Aunt Mary rears up and says, "Listen, you goofs, I've been ready to go for 20 years, when I had my first heart attack and discovered that every new day is a gift. Relax and let me tell you about where I'm going."

Last week, sitting with friends mostly younger than I, I got carried away and held forth about my deepest attitudes toward death. I immediately felt uneasy about what I'd said.

Everyone who's reached my age or older thinks about death, I'm reasonably certain. I didn't when I was younger, because in this time and place most people survive at least into their seventies, and deaths of infants or children seem tragic and unnatural.

Sitting there, I said things that Great Aunt Mary would have understood perfectly, but young people, unless they've walked through the valley of the shadow, often find difficult or obscure.

I explained my belief that the line between life and death is very thin, and that, in some ultimate sense, it doesn't really matter which side I'm on because God is on both sides.

Then I added the corker: some days I find it difficult to care which side I'm on, because on those days it's hard to keep on keeping on.

I suspect that Great Aunt Mary and her peers, and most who have experienced life-threatening illnesses or accidents, know exactly what I mean.

These are normal feelings that need to be acknowledged. Speaking them aloud is a great relief. Yet leaving my friends, I felt I'd spoken the unspeakable.

I love life. I greet most days with a song or psalm. One of my favorites is, "This is the day that the LORD has made; let us rejoice and be glad in it." Psalm 118:24. I sing with gusto, and try to live each day as the treasure it is.

And some days I'm plumb tired, unable to do many of the things I'd like. Then I wonder about the Great Passage.

What Great Aunt Mary knows, and I've also learned, is that God's greatest gift is eternal life. Those who have near-death experiences and reach that thin dividing line but return to this life often speak of seeing amazing things. Their experiences reach across time, cultures, and religions. They tell of a beautiful place, seeing family members and religious figures, and warm, brilliant light that does not hurt their eyes.

They have tasted the reality of Resurrection. They no longer fear death and know that life's purposes are far greater than our daily doings suggest.

This is the Easter message. Behold, He lives! Through Him, we live!

God's Body

Last fall we left most of our fish in the pond, because when Lowell tried to catch them they darted away. He netted only three large goldfish and five minnows. We splashed them into a large bucket and carried them inside. where they happily spent the winter. The others stayed in the pond, which is three feet deep at its deepest part.

We hooked up a pond heater, which was supposed to keep a small area of water unfrozen. When ice covers the whole pond, we were told, toxic gases can collect in the water that will kill the fish. Keeping a small surface area open allows the gases to escape.

By January the ice on our pond looked thick enough to drive a truck over. The ice pushed the heater up so that it looked as if it was sitting mostly on top of the ice. I couldn't see any open water. So much for releasing gases.

In early March Lowell went out to the pond and found a dead fish. He came in looking dejected. "They're probably all dead," he said sadly. He showed me where he had recycled the dead fish as fertilizer among the canes of our outdoor bamboo.

Then, two weeks later, we walked out to the pond and saw, deep in the murky water, eight live fish swimming, four minnows and four goldfish. They looked healthy, apparently unharmed by winter or toxic gases.

Now we've noticed that one of our hardy water lilies in the deepest part of the pond is starting to grow, sending up small pads. The cycle begins again.

One of the best things about our pond is that it's chock full of life. We've seen bugs swimming and skating the surface, and robins and swallows drinking and bathing, slopping water everywhere. I love to sit by the pond and watch. It's a tiny ecosystem and something is always happening, if I have eyes to see.

Such is our world, full of wonders, life and death and

life again. I like to think that the whole thing — the birds and sky, trees and shrubs and the tiniest plants, all the animals including the minutest earthworms, all people and microscopic critters, the earth itself and its water, the building-up and tearing down, all the natural cycles — is really the body of God, with billions of interdependent parts that make up the whole of God's creation.

I love this idea. It lets me see our planet, our universe as a living, breathing entity. The cycles go on endlessly, but as the whole is healthy, we are healthy.

What would happen, I wonder, if most people in the world adopted our world as God's very body? What if all people who say they believe in God — Christians, Jews, Muslims and others — asked themselves, each time they take large or small actions with planetary impact, does what I am about to do honor or dishonor God's body?

I'm guessing that a lot of our decisions would become gentler toward each other, toward all living things and even toward the earth itself.

This is my meditation as I gaze into our pond.

SEASONS OF DISCOVERY

9

The Alphabet of Faith

I've been watching my six-year-old granddaughter learn to read. It's a remarkable process and reminds me that human language is a gift from generations of ancestors in the distant past. I've almost been able to see those generations in her as she's played with language at every stage of her development.

Before she went to kindergarten, this girl could read and write the alphabet, her name and a few other words. Now, at the end of her kindergarten year, her language skills have blossomed. She's read her way through every kindergarten and first grade book. Her teachers and principal have had to invent new reading awards for her.

This has not been without a glitch or two. For the first few months she worked very hard to learn to read. Then she told her mom, in that definitive way young children can have, "I don't want to read any more." She didn't want to be read to either.

Mom, being smart and supportive, understood not to push. Soon the problem was revealed. Darling granddaughter had found that learning to read was harder than she'd anticipated. It required hours spent sounding out words and attaching them to meanings. It required making sense of whole sentences. Her progress, though substantial, wasn't fast and effortless enough to suit her.

Happily, she decided to persevere.

I can relate to my granddaughter's struggle. Sometimes, in my spiritual life, I hit a plateau — which, after I come to terms with continued efforts seemingly without results, is usually all right for a while, a nice spell of quietly catching up with myself. Consolidating gains, I'd like to think.

Other times, I take one step forward and two back. Then my loose ends start unraveling again, and challenges that I can't quite seem to handle crop up all around me. Sometimes this happens when I start thinking I'm doing pretty well in my spiritual life, and these new challenges show me just how full of self-deception I can be. It's usually a struggle to get back on the path. The reward is that, as I do, both my Christian understanding and my desire to please God grow deeper and more vital.

My ultimate goal is to become more like Jesus in my daily life. This is what I understand as salvation in this life, here and now. It happens as I, through God's grace, become kinder, gentler, more patient, more generous, peaceful and joyful. Not to mention more forgiving, courageous and faithful.

Like my granddaughter learning to read, I've discovered that my spiritual task is much harder than I ever thought it could be. Like her, I'm surrounded by support. She perseveres because no matter how unhappy she might be about her progress, no matter how far from the goal she thinks herself to be, her parents and teacher remind her of how much she's learned. My reminders come from family, friends, church community, and above all God, who has a way of breaking into my complacency and showing me what I need to see.

The increasing joy in my life is enough to keep me on the path. Joy in God, in life generally and in other people — I've come to think this is the best part of my life.

My seasons of discovery are the times when I have the courage to keep moving, learning things about myself, about others and life, about relating to God that I could not have imagined before. This renews and refreshes me. Often the seasons of discovery are seasons of darkness that can be deeply painful. Out of these comes the light of grace and new life.

As my granddaughter is learning and I continue to learn, nothing worth doing is ever quite easy. There are always new challenges, new vistas. Thank you, God, for a life of growth and invitation.

Rejoice, It's Advent

Tomorrow is the first Sunday of Advent, and there is something in me — something wild, from the north country, all frozen ground and biting wind — that loves how dusk falls early now, in golds, pinks and purples over our valley. It falls over our garden too, over the autumn beauty of the pines and spruce, the bare-limbed snow crabs and apricot trees, the red and yellow-stemmed dogwood. Even the asters and mums have given up their vibrant colors and turned brown, going underground to rest and recuperate until next spring. The air crackles with cold and snow appears on our mountains.

From my study window I see the lights of town in the distance and I'm drawn to them. When I retired from ministry in Colorado and returned here to Montana, my husband Lowell still had eight more months to pastor his church there. My first Advent back home I was alone, and

I'd sit watching how night slipped down and veiled the landscape. I was joyful at being here, yet teary at the long wait until my sweetheart of four decades could join me.

Advent is like that for me, a time of light and dark, joy and waiting. Like most of us, I revel in Christmas preparations, putting up the tree, watching lights appear in neighborhoods and wondering if they'll be as beautiful this year as last.

The light is special because right around Christmas is the darkest part of the year, with the shortest days. I think it's no accident that many cultures celebrate with light during this dark season.

For Christians, our celebration is the birth of Jesus, who is our "way, truth, light." Jesus came to walk with us on earth and show us how God calls us to treat each other. "I want to walk as a child of the light," we sing.

Advent is our time of waiting for this glorious birth. Henri Nouwen calls it "active waiting" because there are spiritual tasks for us to undertake.

One of these is to look honestly and searchingly into our own hearts. Like the darkness in our Advent days, I see much darkness in myself. Some is good. It's a place I go to rest and heal. Some isn't so good. It's where I store my hurts, anger and denial. "Sure I did enough for the victims of Hurricane Katrina." "Why shouldn't I be mad at the guy who cut me off in traffic?" "I won't forgive her. What she said was very cutting."

The look inside isn't pleasant, but to grow spiritually it's necessary. The next step is to accept the good in me — the ways I yearn and work for the light — and then to admit the wrongs I've done and ask God for forgiveness. That's when my soul opens, the light pours in, and I too find myself standing awe-struck at the manger saying, "Oh, wonder, oh, joy, come and see what our God has done for us!"

Attending Christmas

When our youngest child was five, he approached his daddy and asked for money. Daddy said, "What do you need money for, you little shrimp?" Our child replied, "Spending is living."

"Oh," we moaned, "our poor five-year-old is already lost to the lure of commercialism. We've failed him."

Unfortunately we were looking not at our child but at our own attitudes. This was a child of outstanding generosity, not to mention imagination. He loved to give gifts and he was an exceptional gift-giver because he had a special talent for finding the perfect gift for someone. Our house tells the story of past years: the pictures he drew that I framed, the living room clock, the matching tableware when we only had odds and ends.

He was also a great giver of compliments. He unfailingly noticed when Mommy had a new hairdo or teacher a new dress, and he said so. He had such an eye for this that his daddy learned to do the same thing. Daddy says to me, "You're so beautiful," and I melt. Our children are such great teachers.

What this child showed us, I see now, was loving attentiveness. He took the time to see what was in front of him, and he had the imagination to act in a loving way on what he saw, with a kiss, a smile or a comment.

When he was little, his gifts were small, ceramics, pictures and little things he bought, like the Christmas brooch I still have, a Santa with no eyes left. His gifts were amazingly right on, things that struck a spark in me, that I still cherish. I wish that I'd seen things then as clearly as he did.

As Christmas draws closer, I find myself daydreaming about that child of long ago, my youngest. It's a joy to see him now, a grown man, and I still see occasional flashes of that child in him.

At my age I've learned much, forgotten much, and am beginning to cling to things of real importance.

Loving attentiveness, the thing he made so clear to me, is right up there near the top. It's what allows us to see how a child's eyes light up with imagination, or how we know something is bothering someone who isn't ready to talk about it yet.

Attentiveness tells a person, "I love you," whether it's through the perfect and unexpected gift, or simply taking the time to be present, to listen and engage.

When we're not attentive, it's as if we've given up actually living our lives and are letting them slip away in a blur of busyness. As for me, been there, done too much of that. I lived too many years unable to recall what I had for breakfast, let alone what my husband might really like for Christmas.

Now I've slowed down, and I want to stay slow. I want to de-multi-task and savor life with a kind of Zen completeness, living each moment instead of being vaguely aware as it whizzes by in another room.

That is my path to Christmas this year. To attend. To listen for singing angels and whispering children. To savor the faces of everyone I see and spend much time in prayer for us and our world.

The Christ Child is coming. Emanuel, God-with-us. Let us attend. Let us wait attentively and care for each other, knowing love will soon be born again, in Bethlehem and in our hearts.

Journey to Bethlehem

What really connected me to Advent was my beloved mother's death. She died at age sixty-nine, way too young. I'd always thought I'd have many more years with her. At the time, my eldest child was 22 and my youngest 15. The phone rang and my dad said, "Mommy's gone." That was it. My beloved mother vanished from this life into — where? Where do they go, our well-loved departed?

Mom's death brought me face to face with mortality, hers and my own. My big question was, Death and what then?

Some say death is the end. There's no soul and nothing survives.

But Mom's death shook those notions out of me. I began remembering God's promises that I learned as a little girl, promises such as, "I am the life everlasting." Slowly, creakily, my mind began to open, and that year at Advent, after months of intense grieving, I went out alone at night into our back yard and had a vision.

What I saw was myself standing alone, deep in the darkest night in a huge snowy field, staring at the stars with tears running down my face saying, "God, what are you? Where are you?"

I might as well have been sitting beside Mother's grave

crying, "Mommy, Mommy."

I had no idea what was in that darkness. Was it the terror of the abyss that I experienced as young woman struggling to grow up and come to terms with life's difficulties? Was it mere emptiness or some other world filled with malign creatures?

Standing in our dark yard, I realized that for my soul's sake I had to face the mystery. I began, faint-heartedly, to look inward.

That year I returned to church. I felt alienated and half-angry. I encountered marvelous spiritual teachers who guided me, and I discovered layers of sin in myself that made my cheeks burn. These are the sins that St. Paul names: "enmities, strife, jealousy, anger, quarrels, dissensions, factions, envy." Galatians 5:20-21.

I am still unpeeling layers of sin in myself, and yet I can look back and see how far I've come. It's a life's work and truly the Lord's path into my heart is becoming straighter.

When I was a child, Christmas was wonderful. It was about presents and parties, yes, but it was also about something more. Every Christmas Eve I thought I heard the angels singing, and every Christmas morning I somehow expected to find the Christ Child asleep under our tree.

The Christ Child was never there, of course, and after opening presents, the day went flat for me. I didn't know then that sustaining Christmas throughout the year was all about serious Advent preparation, which to me means opening the heart to God and letting God inside to cleanse and heal.

Advent for me is my personal journey to Bethlehem, to stand again in awe and wonder at the manger. Tomorrow is the first Sunday in Advent. It's a wonderful time. Let our prayers begin.

All-Day Sucker

Today was the big day, the day we got out for Christmas vacation, when the class exchanged small gifts right before we went home.

I was in the fifth grade in Miss Woodburn's classroom. I remember the old steam radiator clanking under the window, overheating the room as usual. Our scraggly Christmas tree sat in front of the blackboard near Miss Woodburn's desk. The tree had no lights, but it was crammed with our class's colored-paper decorations and I thought it beautiful.

As I slipped into my seat, an old-fashioned desk with a top that opened to stow books inside, my eyes fixed on the gaily wrapped presents hanging on and lying under the tree. I thought the silver-wrapped lacy hanky I brought looked especially enticing.

The class was boisterous with excitement, but Miss Woodburn silenced us with "the look." "The look" said, "One more loud noise and this class stays after school for ten minutes." It warned us with what seemed like imprisonment for eternity. There was utter silence. Nobody seemed to breathe.

But even while I settled into my seat, my eyes fixed on this huge thing on the Christmas tree. It dangled there unwrapped, ugly, all whitish with a few pale green and red streaks through it, and one white ribbon dangling from the handle. It was an all-day sucker that looked so sweet it would make you sick, the kind I couldn't stand.

I stared at that sucker as a boy in the class passed out the gifts, and I knew, I just knew, that sucker was for me. My eyes darted to the other brightly wrapped packages, cologne or comb-and-brush sets for the girls, balsam wood model airplanes and toy cars for the boys, and there dangled that sucker.

I had to wait through half the alphabet, since my last name started with "M." I know my cheeks were already flaming when, with a pitying glance, that boy thrust the monster sucker at me.

I wanted to disappear inside my desk or through the floor. While the other kids laughed and tore open their wrappings, I was alone on another planet where that sucker stared up at me from my desk. I couldn't bear to touch it. I didn't want to show it to my mother, who was waiting outside for me.

Finally I was the last kid left in the classroom and Miss Woodburn smiled at me, picked up her purse and said, "Merry Christmas, Joan."

I knew I had to go. I stuffed the sucker in my coat pocket and trudged bravely out of the school. I showed the sucker to Mom. She understood the expression on my face and murmured, "Oh, honey, I'm sorry."

I never tasted that sucker. I dropped it in my bottom drawer with old socks I never wore. A few years later I found it melted into the socks.

Why did I feel so upset by that silly all-day sucker? Now I realize it might have been the best some struggling family could afford. Or maybe the child who brought it really loved that kind of suckers. It probably wasn't personal — how could anyone know that I was revolted by such cloyingly sweet candy?

Maybe it's for the best that public schools don't do gift exchanges like that anymore. Too many opportunities for children to feel as I did, embarrassed and humiliated. Because of course at the time I did think it was personal.

So now I have a Christmas wish for all of us. If some

all-day sucker or its equivalent is still floating around out there, here's hoping it finds its way only to someone who will truly cherish it.

Touching Ashes

Remember the old children's rhyme, "Ring around the rosy, pocket full of posy, ashes, ashes, all fall down"? In my seminary sacred dance class, we danced Ring-Around-the-Rosy scattering rose petals and dropping to the floor on, "Ashes, ashes, all fall down."

In medieval times, rose petals were used to mask the smell of the black plague. Ashes represented the burned bodies of its victims. My encyclopedia says the plague killed as many as three-quarters of the European and Asian populations. Now it's embedded in a children's rhyme.

On Ash Wednesday I attended a service to mark the beginning of Lent, the forty days before Easter when we Christians prepare our souls anew for the glory of the Resurrection. The pastor's murmured, "From ashes you come, to ashes you will return," and the ashes on my forehead recalled the nursery rhyme.

Lent is a time to remember our mortality, not to be morbid but to remind us to live life to the fullest. Lent is thus also a time of joy. Babies are born every day, and people recover from ghastly illnesses or injuries. All around us is nature's abundant beauty. I have only to lift my eyes. I can curl my fingers around a dogwood twig and feel the pulse of new life. In a few weeks the air will soften and spring will leap into green. My heart sings with affirmations: Life is good! Spring is coming!

Still, much of life remains a mystery. Why did God give us a world with illness and death? Why couldn't God give us a world of only joy and beauty?

The ancient Hebrews answered that question with the story of Adam and Eve in Eden, where God provided for all their needs. They sinned, thus falling from grace, so God chased them out into this world's difficult challenges.

I wonder, though, whether God didn't want something more demanding from people than "just say no" to the fruit of a single tree. God gave us this incredibly lovely world and said, "It is good. Take care of it." God created us in God's own image, and said, in effect, "Love me and love each other so that you establish my Kingdom here on earth. I gave you everything you need. Now get busy."

Jesus came to show us love in human acts and words, teaching us again and again about God's Kingdom.

Ash Wednesday and Lent remind us that we've failed to establish God's Kingdom here, and that we need to repent and do better. It's not likely that we humans can ever eradicate death, no matter how advanced our medical science. But we can do great things by helping others make good lives.

At the end of Lent stands Easter, when we celebrate Jesus' Resurrection, another mystery and a part of God's Kingdom. With all its wonders, Resurrection is in God's hands. As for me, my place is to keep working for God's Kingdom, that here-and-now place of love, peace and justice for all God's creatures.

Crucifixions

Next Friday Christians observe the anniversary of Jesus' crucifixion. Crucifixion is about death, but it's also about the new life that can happen when the old, the untransformed, passes away.

My favorite personal "crucifixion" story happened when I was a pastor in a 500-member congregation in a booming suburban area. New buildings were going up all around us, and nearby churches were flourishing.

But our church had stagnated. We had a bogged-down building project, flagging attendance and a dispirited congregation. I was new, and through prayer received a powerful vision for change. My vision showed me what that church could be, a beacon of the Gospel, a center for growth and healing, a place to encounter God.

I pitched my vision to as many people as I could, as often as I could. I probably never shut up.

And, well, there were barriers. Attitudes. Maybe you've heard them. "Tried that and it didn't work." "We've never done it that way before." "We don't have the money."

I kept raising the vision, the congregation grew restless then angry, and I knew what was coming. I didn't know the day or hour, but I was going to be hoisted on the petard of my lovely church vision. One definition of petard, by the way, is a case of explosives used to break down a door or wall.

The petard blew one night after a long, painful meeting. When it did, I was not bleeding, but I felt as if I were. I reached my study in tears. That petard blew me and the other pastor right out of that church.

But, more importantly, it blew down those barriers to change and growth.

I recently visited that church. It has a stunningly beautiful new sanctuary and is growing the way it should. It is full of life and love. The pastor showed me around and knew a bit of the story. He said, "This is your blood, sweat and tears."

I walked out with a different kind of tears in my eyes. For me it was a moment of unalloyed grace.

I knew what I was doing during those difficult days. I believed, and still do, that God had sent me there for that very reason, because God knew I had the strength, the persistence and maybe enough just pure orneriness to keep pushing.

Then boom! The petard blew and I was gone.

And that was okay. It happened the way it needed to.

I think I was a tiny bit like Jesus in those days, though he was a thousand times more so. He went to Jerusalem, right into the temple to teach his wonderful Gospel of God's love. He pushed the Jerusalem authorities as far as he could, and I think he knew what would happen. You don't speak the truth to power without powerful people getting angry. Sometimes powerful people kill.

I wasn't really crucified. I didn't even bleed.

Jesus was. And his body died. And his Spirit and his love live forever.

Running the Risks

One sultry summer afternoon when I was about nine years old, my mother refused to take me swimming. I rebelled and scraped together enough change from my allowance and under sofa cushions to buy a bus ticket. Away I went across town, running off to an unsanctioned afternoon of fun in the pool.

Except that I transferred to the wrong bus and ended up in a totally unfamiliar place. I saw that I was lost and then I got frightened. I found a small Mom-and-Pop grocery where a kind lady let me call home. I was so relieved when Mom arrived to pick me up. She hugged me, then scolded and grounded me. And that scary adventure, small as it was, opened me up to a whole world of exciting possibilities.

I've run quite a few times since then and I've concluded that sometimes running makes sense. I've run from a high school I found bone-wearyingly dull, from a God I identified too closely with my dad, from an abusive marriage. More significantly, I've run to many wonderful things: to schools I loved; to marriage with a man who seemed so different from me and yet has become my soulmate; to a new grace-filled relationship with God; and finally, marvelously, to ministry.

The Bible has plenty of examples of people running from and to important things. Jonah ran from God's call to go tell the people of Nineveh that God wanted them to repent, and that God would punish them if they didn't.

Jonah was such a successful prophet that he converted the sailors on the ship he took to escape his Ninevah mission. God was not pleased when Jonah tried to run away, and he sent a terrible storm. Jonah knew the storm was about his disobedience, and he told the sailors to save themselves by tossing him into the sea.

God sent a great fish to gobble Jonah up, and Jonah spent three days in the fish's belly. Then he was spat up on dry land. By then Jonah was willing to obey God, and he ran to Nineveh, where he convinced the whole city to repent, even the animals.

Jonah was the grumpy, reluctant prophet whose running only took him to God's intended destination.

One day Jesus went to the seashore and called the fishermen Simon, Andrew, James and John, and they heard him and ran after him to become his disciples. I'm sure none of them had any idea how wonderful and difficult that would be, especially when God called Jesus to run to Jerusalem where he would be crucified.

Running both from and to things can be risky and dangerous. Sometimes, like Jonah, you try to run away and can't, and end up doing God's work against your will. Other times you run to something and find that you have, metaphysically speaking, a tiger by the tail.

But staying in the same place for too long can be deadly to spiritual health. God calls us, I believe, to stretch, reach and sometimes to run. God called both my husband and me to run to seminary and ministry, a joyous time in my life.

The truth is, I suspect, that the body can always remain in the same physical location. But I believe that the soul, the living spirit, has first to listen, then to run and finally to take wing.

Don't See Me Now

A few years ago my best friend's four-year-old granddaughter used to dash through the house giggling and shrieking, "Don't see me now!"

The girl's mother would sigh, "She's up to something. I better check."

Once she drenched the silverware drawer with Mom's new hand cream. Another time she wrote her name in colorful markers all over the kitchen cabinets. Her mom was not amused, though my friend and I had a hard time not laughing.

My laughter, I think, was because there was something so familiar about the little girl's loud cry while she went wildly charging past us. Don't, oh please don't, see me now.

I remember, back in the day, being that little girl. There was the time I jumped off the neighbors' shed roof into a huge mud puddle and went home muddy from head to toe.

And the time I asked my grandma what her pretty red pills tasted like. To me they looked like yummy, cinnamony red hots.

"Why, honey, they don't really taste like anything," Grandma said. I couldn't understand how something couldn't taste like anything, so the first chance I got I started swallowing them. And got my stomach pumped.

As I grew older, I continued this pattern of doing something wrong or at least questionable, then trying to hide it and evade the consequences.

When I was at Cornell College in Iowa, we freshman girls had 8:30 curfews on weekdays. My friend Delores used to lend me her car so I could sneak down the fire escape in the wee hours and drive to the all-night library at the University of Iowa about 24 miles away.

Sometimes I'd sit for hours in a nearby café, drinking coffee and studying, feeling bold and adventurous, knowing very well that if caught, I could get kicked out of school. I usually didn't return until almost dawn.

Don't see me now. I have plenty more examples of this, running through half my life.

Then one day I finally began to understand what Jesus meant when he said, "For nothing is hidden that will not be disclosed, nor is anything secret that will not become known and come to light." Luke 8:17.

I began to stumble toward the value of spiritual transparency, when the heart opens to God and yearns to be fully known with nothing hidden.

As the Psalmist says, "Search me, O God, and know my heart…" Psalm 139:23.

This was a major spiritual breakthrough, when I began letting go my own "Don't see me now," and my heart began yearning for transparency with God. Transparency, I discovered, is a critical step toward transformation in Christ. Increasingly I understood that nothing less would do.

I am not fully transparent now, but I am mostly so. "Don't see me now" is a growth phase for little kids. But to be mature in the Lord, the time comes when we have to say, "Yes, Lord, see everything inside, so that I may be transformed into your likeness."

~At the Water's Edge~

HOLY HAPPINESS

10

Feasting on Small Things

I recall when I was a young mother, living in the first house we owned, a small, pretty white house with a green hip roof, in Iowa City, Iowa. We lived there when our youngest child was born, a son, and we already had an older son and two daughters.

Off the kitchen was a small room, maybe seven by nine feet. It was probably once a pantry, though when my husband and I bought the house the little room had no shelves. We used it by piling bags of canned goods and other stuff in there.

The important thing about that little room to me was that it had no windows. It was entirely on the interior of the house. It felt safe.

Thunder storms in Iowa City were magnificent and

sometimes frightening. During the Second World War when my mother and I lived in Iowa City with my grandparents, Grandma Carlton used to say, when the lightning ripped and the thunder rolled, that it was just old Mr. McGillicuddy driving his wagon over the old wooden bridge. As a child I was not afraid of lightning and thunder.

But those early years of motherhood when my eldest was seven and my youngest a newborn, I was afraid of so many things. Of not being a competent mom. Of being an inadequate wife. Of not having enough money to make ends meet. Much of this was just undifferentiated anxiety — at the time I really didn't know what it was about.

But I did know, when the lightning crashed overhead and took out the chimney of the house across the alley and only two doors down, that I was afraid of the storm. That day I took all the children into that little room and huddled in there holding them for maybe half an hour while the storm was at its peak.

I've come a long way since then. Even Iowa storms don't frighten me that way anymore. I recall maybe fifteen years ago tent camping in a state park not far from where I grew up. The storm came and the lightning raged, and as soon as it started I said, "Let's sit in the car until it's over. It's not safe in the tent." I'd heard too many stories of what lightning can do, including the time it struck my uncle's windmill and traveled through the plumbing of the whole farmhouse. Fortunately nobody was bathing or washing dishes. "We would have been electrocuted," my aunt said.

So, prudent, we waited out the storm in the car. But I wasn't afraid and I didn't huddle. I rather enjoyed it.

And the free-floating anxiety that stayed with me for many years is pretty much gone now.

Through years of learning to listen for God, of giving over my feelings of helplessness, hopelessness and fear, I've let peace and joy come into my life.

Most days my heart sings with happiness. For me happiness is biblical, in the sense the Psalmist uses the word "happy" in Psalm One.

> Happy are those
> who do not follow the advice of the wicked,
> Or take the path that sinners tread,
> or sit in the seat of scoffers;
> But their delight is in the law of the Lord,
> and on his law they meditate day and night.
> They are like trees
> planted by streams of water,
> which yield their fruit in its season,
> and their leaves do not wither. Psalm 1:1-3a

Happiness, I'm convinced, has to do with aligning ourselves, inside and out, with the movements of God's universe. It's about our relationship with the God in whom "we live and move and have our being." Acts 17:28.

It has to do with striving to live in accord with Jesus' teachings, both with the things he said and the lessons of his life. It's about turning to God and giving over our lives, learning to walk with God, with Jesus, every step of the way.

Above all, my happiness manifests in simple things. In taking a hot shower, or the way my husband throws back his head and roars with laughter when something really grabs his funny bone. In the arching branches of our Persian Copper roses as they put on buds outside my window, preparing for the early summer show. In a shaft of sunlight on our breakfast table, giving the wood — and my opening heart — a golden glow.

Most days, life is a feast of such small yet vital things.

It is of these that holy happiness is made. My prayer is that someday the whole wide world will know this happiness.

Night of Wonder, Awe and Upchuck

On Christmas Eve afternoons when I was a girl, my excitement spiked when my family and I drove twenty-three miles to pick up Grandma.

When we arrived home, Mom and Grandma would start supper, and my dad and I would drive around town to deliver Christmas hams to his employees. When we returned, supper was ready, my very favorite, chicken with thick and chewy noodles made only with egg, flour and a little salt. "No water," Grandma always said, "that makes them slick." I learned to make those noodles — which my own children renamed "blubber noodles."

After supper my anticipation surged as we staged our family Christmas program, mainly me reciting, "The Night Before Christmas" and reading Luke's Christmas story. Then we'd dress up and attend our always magical eleven o'clock Christmas Eve service. As the choir sang, mysteriously I'd be certain I heard echoes of the heavenly host, and at the end we'd sing "Silent Night" by flickering candlelight.

At midnight we'd spill into the crisp, chill air, sometimes with snow falling, and everybody would cry, "Merry

Christmas." The world felt bright and new, ripe with promise, and I knew I heard the angels singing.

At home I'd jump into my pajamas, put out cookies and milk for Santa, who was still as real to me as the singing angels, and hop into bed. By then Grandma, who shared my room when she visited, would unpin the long braid she wore wound around the back of her head. She'd unbraid it, brush it out, rebraid it and climb under the covers.

That was when — every year — it happened. I'd make a beeline for the bathroom where I'd throw up from sheer anticipation. "Well, Joanie," Grandma would say, "maybe Christmas wouldn't come without that."

When my children were young, I still retained most of my Christmas excitement, awe, wonder and anticipation — though I didn't upchuck anymore. But as the years passed, I lost it all. For years I spent Christmas skeptical and railing against commercialism, feeling more annoyance than joy about the season.

Those were the years during which I abandoned the church, thinking I could leave God behind, didn't need God, didn't need Jesus. I was so young and tough. Even so, I prayed for my children every night — so go figure.

Then, one bright day, my husband and I returned to a warm, welcoming church — and wonder of wonders, all the excitement, awe, and mystery of the angel appearing to

Mary and the birth of the Christ Child were restored to me. It grows in me every year, and now I know I hear the heavenly host on Christmas Eve. I know too that love will be born anew in my heart on Christmas morning. The baby Jesus comes to refresh my weary spirit, to give wings to my soul, and to infuse more love into my anxious heart.

How marvelous — God's perfect Christmas gift.

Blue Christmases

Recently I was in a group of friends when the conversation turned to the painful part of Christmas. A new widow said, "I put up a good front for the sake of my family, but some days I don't think I can go on." "My grandson has leukemia," a grandfather said. "I watch my wife cry with my heart breaking." I also know a daughter seeing her father disappear into Alzheimer's, a mother hoping her son will be home soon from Iraq, and a family where no matter how hard or how much the parents work seems to pull the family out of poverty.

Hearts break sometimes even a little faster at Christmas time, and it's easy to assume that others are living the storybook Christmas while we are not.

I hope everyone has a storybook Christmas this and every year, but we all know that doesn't happen. Some

Christmases are simply a torment. The bells don't jingle, the lights are dim, and Santa's laughter sounds more sinister than jolly.

"It feels like I'm entering a desert," a father said as his son was born many months prematurely.

Having recently, during my heart surgery and early months of recovery, been in a vast desert, I answered, "Go there." In my desert I was helpless, like that baby born anew to us tomorrow morning. I had no control over anything, including whether I lived or died. I had no choice but to surrender.

When I did, I found myself in the arms of a loving God who wrapped me in the most incredible peace and never left me.

We have so little control over the most important things in life. Of course we can do many things, but when the chips are down, we cannot bargain death away or change the course another person has chosen.

"I'm afraid if I let go," my friend Liana once said, "everything will fall apart. I have to hold it together."

Sometimes life makes us feel so broken and hopeless. In the desert of our brokenness God stands ready to embrace us, to comfort us and strengthen us for life's journey, a journey that God walks with us.

The thing to remember is that the desert is always a

beginning, never the end. Jesus went into the desert for forty days at the start of his ministry. He came out strengthened and renewed.

You've probably heard the old saying, "Let go and let God." To me it means surrender and enter the desert, knowing we will find there the One who helps us discover the answers we need, and offers us enough strength to buoy us up for the rest of our lives.

Tomorrow the Christ Child comes again, born into a beautiful God-given world that is nevertheless full of suffering. If this Christmas is difficult, remember that God waits in the desert for our surrender. Christmas will always come again. That's the wonder of it. Hallelujah and amen.

Angel Wings

Two weeks ago my four-year-old granddaughter had a mad on when her mommy brought her to church. I didn't realize how she was feeling. I came into the sanctuary while the children were practicing their Christmas pageant.

Our little darling refused to practice and when church started she wouldn't go to Sunday school with her brother and the other kids. She curled up on the floor against the wall, a few feet away from her mother and me, with this small mushed up face. Every now and then she'd come over and climb on her mom's lap, then she'd give each of us a dirty look and go back to her pile of ashes against the wall.

After a while she cheered up and was as sweet as she could be.

Driving home with my husband, I said, "She was sure torqued about something this morning."

He said, "I heard that somebody lost her angel wings for the pageant." Oh.

Midweek I talked to her mom, who said, "I was the one who lost the wings, but I've found them."

So last Sunday morning there she was, angel wings and bright little face, singing her heart out in the pageant. Her seven-year-old brother had a solo and sang wonderfully with his pure, high voice, looking angelic as he always does, no matter what he's up to. Pastor Grandpa beamed from the pulpit and I, the grandma, beamed from the pews.

Our little granddaughter was the littlest angel by far, except for the lovely infant girl who played the Christ Child. This baby lay in the manger in front of the plastic Mary and Joseph, watching everything with big wonder-filled eyes. She never let out a peep during the pageant. "The little Lord Jesus, no crying (s)he makes."

These simple homespun church events brought back a memory of when I, in seventh grade, got to play the littlest angel in my school's play, The Star of Bethlehem. I was so excited that I almost threw up back stage.

My friend Karl was the boy lead. At the end just as the curtain was closing, Karl's eyes rolled and his mouth fell open with his tongue sticking out. I couldn't see him, but the audience roared. As if he were saying, "Thank heaven it's over," my mom commented afterwards.

Our grandchildren at church and my own memories awakened the little angel inside me. I think a little angel is in each of us, the innocence of our childhoods, though as the years pass it's easy to forget and leave the angelic child sleeping.

These little angels are precious gifts from God. They are our inner children, of whom Jesus said, "Let the little ones come to me." They are holy, full of grace, and, no matter how battered by life, still utterly precious in God's sight.

Awake, awake, little angels. In a few days we'll stand again at the manger, gazing with awe at the Christ Child. Come let us adore Him.

Making Joyful Noises

This Advent has been wonderful for me, full of music and children's pageants. I was feeling so good and, because I love to sing, the Holy Spirit moved me to join my husband's church choir. Our gracious director said, "Yes."

~At the Water's Edge~

Wow —

The truth is, I have no voice. A chorus of frogs can do better. When I open my mouth to sing often nothing comes out. Other times I barely croak. It takes three or four measures before I make anything resembling a musical tone.

I sing alto, because I can no longer reach the high notes, and on the lower notes my voice is hoarse and raspy. No boon to the choir, I'm afraid. Plus I'm easily confused on the alto part, though I work hard at it and it runs non-stop through my head all day long.

Yet singing for me is pure joy, especially during Advent and Christmas. While singing joyful music, loud, soft, lullaby or triumphant carol, I feel the Holy Spirit moving, breathing new life into me, into all of us.

The Holy Spirit is central at this time of year. It is God's Spirit, God's power, that overshadows Mary and gives her the divine baby, our Emanuel, God-with-us, our Jesus Christ who is both completely human and completely divine at the same time, one of the eternal mysteries of the Christian faith.

It is God's Spirit born in a stable as the grace-filled infant Jesus, the child who grows up to show us the possibility of human perfection, even to the point of death. Jesus is so full of God's Spirit that to see him is to see God in action.

~Holy Happiness~

God's Spirit, I believe, is breathed into each of us at birth. The Spirit makes us capable of raising joyful noises to God, building glorious cathedrals and doing great works of compassion for others.

So last Wednesday evening was our choir cantata, a lovely piece combining original and traditional music. The Holy Spirit was definitely at work because I remembered most of my part, and of course the others were terrific. A marvelous evening was had by choir and audience alike.

It's no accident that some of our greatest music evokes God's Spirit. I'm certain that the Holy Spirit inspired it in the first place.

Every year during this season the Holy Spirit moves in me in a special way. Somehow, even if I start out feeling weary and broken, the Spirit renews me. Each year I do the same Advent activities: I help Lowell set up our collection of Nativity scenes and our now 16-year-old Christmas tree, and I sing the same carols.

And every year it feels like my first Christmas. What happens, I think, is that each year the Spirit opens my heart wider and I let God embrace me more fully.

And my heart sings. And my mouth sings. To my human friends I may croak like a chorus of frogs, but I am assured that God hears only the purest, clearest of joyful noises.

Everyday Resurrections

A small resurrection is when my five-year-old grand-daughter calls to tell me that the flower seeds she planted last week are up. What joy! She waited hard, her mom says, upset that the seeds didn't pop up right away. Resurrection is often about waiting.

Another small resurrection is when my east coast daughter calls to tell me that her newly licensed sixteen-year-old son has gone off on his first solo drive to the video store with his younger brother. "Talk to me until they're back," she says anxiously. Sometimes resurrection contains a little terror.

A bigger resurrection happened right after New Year's 1982. The Honolulu coroner called my brother John in Iowa to say that our father, Colonel McAllister, had gone swimming in Waikiki, had pulled himself up on a raft, had a heart attack and died. A clerk at the Hale Koa military hotel where he'd been staying identified the body. It was being prepared for shipment home to Iowa.

I was working late and my husband Lowell got John's call. By the time I arrived home, John had called back with the good news: Dad was alive and well, but hadn't been located yet. John had phoned our Aunt Helen in California, who said, "Oh, honey, your dad came here for the Rose

Bowl game. I put him on a plane back to Honolulu two days ago. If that man's been dead a week, he isn't your father."

So from the start my head knew that Dad was alive, supposedly staying at Bellows Field on Oahu. But my mother had died of a massive coronary the past May, and the thought of losing Dad so soon was agony. I paced bleakly back and forth in our kitchen, dragging wads of hankies and a long phone cord — we didn't have wireless in those days — calling Bellows Field again and again, and talking endlessly to Lowell and John and Helen, who tried but were unable to reassure me.

My heart was already grieving my dad. I couldn't settle down or truly believe he was alive until I heard his voice. It was an exhausting evening. Finally about 1 p.m. Montana time he called back.

He'd gone out to dinner and then strolled leisurely along the beautiful Bellows Field beach. I was laughing and crying, incredibly happy. I remember hoping the coroner would be able to identify the poor man in the morgue.

This experience was a pale version of what Mary Magdalene felt when the risen Christ identified himself to her. It was a tiny bit like when Doubting Thomas would not, could not, believe in the Resurrection until he stuck his fingers into Jesus' wounds.

Jesus' Resurrection is the unique and original one, the template for all resurrections large and small. It taught us, so wonderfully and mysteriously, not to fear death, and always to look for new beginnings, never the end.

So I say, resurrections are all around us. We need only have the eyes to see.

Notes on a Birth: From God's Heart to Us

In 1981, shortly after my mother died, I went out into our yard. I was still grieving hard for her, and it was December, a dark and frigid night. I had a vision that night which has stayed with me all these years. Slowly it has unfolded its meanings to me, and now I recognize it as a significant page in the book of my life.

I saw myself as a young girl standing alone, in the midst of darkest night, in a huge snowy field that seemed to go on forever. I was staring up at the stars with tears running down my face, and I was saying, "God, what are you? Where are you?"

I was crying out to God and yet I felt as if I, a forty-one-year-old woman, were sitting at my mother's grave crying, "Mommy, Mommy."

~Holy Happiness~

I have come to see the impulse of crying out to God as very similar to calling for a beloved parent. "Where are you?" "Have you forgotten me?" "Why don't you come and take care of me?"

Eventually I began to understand that my vision, of me alone in the cold and dark, crying out, is primal. I came to see it as part of the human condition. We are abruptly expelled from the comfort of the womb into a cold and strange world. To me this expulsion is a kind of parallel to God driving the First Couple from Eden and never allowing them to return.

For me personally my vision tells me about a newborn baby girl taken at birth in 1939 for adoption, and placed for almost three months in an orphanage, lying helpless in an iron crib screaming for attention.

Please understand that I don't know this earliest part of my own history for a fact. It is what I believe based on my growing knowledge of myself, and it is what I think based on my historical knowledge of orphanages at that time, places that were so underfunded and understaffed that they could barely keep their babies alive.

That primal me lay submerged, completely hidden from my conscious mind, for many years. I'm sure others could see parts of it in me, in my many insecurities that arose from my early difficult months. But to me that early history was a blank wall, a house with no doors or windows. When Lowell and I were first married, he asked:

"Why don't you ever write about your childhood, Joan?"

Shocked, I said, "I can't remember." I couldn't, but the truth was, I didn't want to. I didn't know what was in that windowless, doorless house, and I feared it.

Then, that cold December night in the darkness, I caught a glimpse of the primal me crying to God. I could hardly stand to look at that frightened young self, but soon after that night certain odd sorts of memories, images of myself, began to emerge.

I saw the inside of that iron crib as if I were lying in it. I was cold, hungry and wet, and my baby arms and legs were flailing. I was squalling for attention.

Are these memories real? Possibly. Emotionally they feel real. Or perhaps God sent these images to me, to tell me who I am and how I can heal.

Not long after that, I bought myself a baby doll, dressed her in a real baby gown and blanket, and held her, rocked her, and crooned to her. "I'm here, baby," I whispered over and over. "I'm here and I won't ever let you go." I did what I could to nurture that surrogate of my baby self, to fill my unmet need during those brief but important months of my life. I wanted to free myself from all that residual pain and fear so that I could learn to love more fully.

Strange as this may sound, nurturing that baby doll helped me. One of the great barriers between ourselves and God, I believe, one of the reasons we sometimes run from full relationship with God, is that we have not truly faced the most painful part of our pasts, and learned, by uncovering whatever is there, to love even the wounded parts of ourselves.

That little doll helped me look back — in sadness, love and fear — at all those years of wondering who I was and whether I really belonged to my family. Slowly I began to look at the baby Joan. Who was she? On some level she had always frightened me. I wonder now if I blamed her, my own helpless baby self, for being so unlovable that her flesh-and-blood mother had dumped her in a cruel and frightening nowhere.

That baby accused me, the adult me, and I began to understand why as a child I hated to look at my infant self, all the while pretending interest to the adults who insisted on showing me those photos.

That baby accused me because she and I were one. We were both despised and responsible for our mutual abandonment. "What is wrong with you?" she seemed to say. "Why are you so unlovable? Why were you abandoned?"

No way in the world would I let myself encounter that accusing baby face.

Until I picked up my doll. And while I cuddled and rocked her, I could barely look at her. Barely look at me.

It was a tiny first step. Yet, small as it was, almost miraculously it began a new stage in my journey to God. In turn that new stage released a bit more of my ability to love in the here and now.

Some years after that, as my December vision of myself stayed alive in my mind, I began connecting it with Mary, mother of Jesus. For the longest time I didn't know why. We Protestants don't usually honor Mary the way Catholics do, and I grew up without a strong attachment to Mary. I only knew that I started seeing Mary as a young girl, pregnant, standing in the snow looking up at the stars of Judea.

What did she see? Did she feel abandoned or unloved in spite of her earlier assent? Was she as human as I — where are you, God? What are you? What will happen to my baby and me?

I have four children. My eldest was born when I was barely nineteen, and thus I also know something about being young and pregnant. I was newly married, rushing into life, foolish and scared. I had not intended to become pregnant when I did. In those days, life just seemed to happen to me.

Mary's situation was in many ways very different from mine, and very risky. She was unmarried, a virgin, overshadowed by the Divine, and she had assented to bear the child of the Divine. Only by the intercession of an angel did Joseph, her betrothed, go ahead and marry her instead of casting her out. She was in a land where even today unmarried girls who become pregnant are sometimes stoned to death.

Being young and pregnant was scary even in the American Midwest of the 1950s. Thinking about it reminded me of the woman I had almost banished from my mind, my own birth mother, the one who gave me up for adoption.

Was she the young girl standing in the December snow looking up at the stars? Was she crying out as I did? Where are you? What are you?

I was born in July, so in December the fact of her pregnancy may just have been dawning on her. As I see her in my vision, I wonder: Was she a girl from a good home who just happened to go too far with her boyfriend? Did she have a boyfriend who wouldn't stop when she said no?

Or was she, as my dad once told me, a chorus girl?

Was she stage-struck and too busy finding work as a dancer to have time for a baby? Or did she have a boyfriend back home whom she wanted to return to and marry?

I've never met my birth mother, so I don't know what she went through when she found she was pregnant with me.

Unlike many adoptees, I've never wanted to look for her, or for my biological father. I was adopted when I was a week under three months old by a wonderful couple, Alice and Warren, who became my "real" parents, the only parents I've ever known. As a child I knew my parents were not able to have children. That was a source of sadness in our home, and it was a real joy when finally they were able to adopt John, my brother.

Many years later my dad told me that he was the sterile one. "I had all kinds of tests," he said, "and lots of shots. But they didn't know very much about fertility in those days, and nothing worked. We finally quit trying and found you."

They enveloped me in love. Not love that stifled, but the free-flowing kind that seemed boundless. They healed everything in me that they could. They couldn't know how much was broken in places so deep that even I was hardly aware of them.

Just today I had a vision of my mother, those beautiful

brown eyes and her sweet, loving face, looking at me as she did when I was a child. She was the world to me. So was my dad, so strong and tall and handsome. Between them I thought they knew everything and could do anything.

I bonded with my parents to the extent that even now I can become upset if someone suggests that they are not "really" my parents. Yes, they really are.

My Advent vision began to merge all four of us on that dark, bone-chilling December night: Mary, Mother of God, my birth mother of whom I know so little, my adoptive mother Alice and myself.

Eventually I began to connect with another, deeper understanding of Mary that had entirely eluded me until recently. It is Mary's utter assent to God. When the angel Gabriel appeared to Mary to tell her that God had chosen her to bear the Divine Child, her final words to the angel were, "Here am I, the servant of the Lord; let it be with me according to your word."

Through Mary's assent the Incarnation of Jesus Christ was able to happen. Through Mary's very flesh, the Jesus Son of God, the Christ who was flesh like us came into the world.

I know Mary is often adored for her obedience, but I think Mary's assent was far more than that. It was courageous. It was the willingness to endure whatever her society might do to her because of this child. It was determination to carry out God's will and see it through. It was the utmost love and faith. This Mary, I have to say, was some woman.

This Mary was, in some sense, Everywoman. She was my birth mother, who I hope went on to a good life. She was Alice, my real mother and my adoptive mother, who took me as an infant stranger and shaped so much of who I am. And Mary was me, too, as I stumbled through rearing my children and, and even now, as I continue on my halting journey to and with God.

Through Mary's assent came Jesus our light, our greatest love, and our salvation. Through my birth mother's assent came my life. Through my mother Alice's assent I had a loving home and lots of good nurture. Through my own assent I have four wonderful grown children and five terrific grandchildren. God is good.

Advent is our own journey to meet God on the road to Bethlehem. Advent takes us from our moments of being deeply despairing, frightened, vulnerable or spiritually impoverished into the light of the Divine Incarnation.

The marvelous thing is that God meets us on that road, and I believe God meets us not at the end or in the middle, when we've started to mature spiritually, but at the very beginning of it. I think God walks with us from the start, though we are often not aware of the divine presence until much later when our hearts open sufficiently wide.

Since my vision of my lonely self years ago, I have learned quite a lot.

About Advent I've learned that it's a special time for me when I need to pause in the darkness to reflect and become refreshed. I need to look at the night stars and feel the cold, and rejoice at what our Lord has done for us.

I've also learned that I can intertwine my own life's story with the stories of the people of the Bible, and at Advent those people are usually Jesus and the people surrounding Jesus' birth. When I cradled that dolly surrogate of my infant self, hoping for inner healing, was I thinking of the infant Jesus, born helpless in a manger on a cold winter's night and yet Very God of Very God? Was I learning to understand myself as also a beloved child of God?

My life makes much more sense to me when I let God's light shine into it. Things are illuminated that I don't like, that embarrass and shame me, and I confess that this happens fairly often, and yet I go back and open myself up again and again. I have learned that this is how spiritual growth happens, facing up to who I am as well as who I want to be.

Somewhere on my journey I fell in love with the first chapter of John's Gospel. These are the verses I most often take with me into the darkness of my Advent meditations. Earlier on my Christian journey I didn't understand John's Gospel at all, especially these first verses. I preferred the birth stories in Luke and Matthew, the manger, the angels, shepherds and wise men, and I still love them.

But now John is my favorite. It shows us the light that leads us to meet our God.

And the Word became flesh and lived among us, and we have seen his glory, the glory as of a father's only son, full of grace and truth.
John 1:14.

To order

At the Water's Edge:

God's Grace in Everyday Life

email: joanuda@yahoo.com

call 406 227-7572

or mail your check and mailing address to:

Rice Universe Publishing

P.O. Box 1065

East Helena, MT 59635